THE SHATTERED SELF

Religion and Other Disciplines

A series of books examining interrelations between as many disciplines as possible demands that there be a base from which to work. In all the areas of inquiry by man, there is one contiguous question, that of values and how these values are applied. For this reason, religion was chosen as a natural and useful discipline from which to embark upon an extensive series of interdisciplinary studies.

The series will probe problems that are basic to understanding man and his quest for knowledge. It will be of benefit to both scholars and interested laymen. It will attempt to serve the rapidly disappearing but desperately needed thinker dedicated to the constant expansion of his view—the generalist. Writers in all disciplines are invited to submit proposed manuscripts. The requirements are two-fold: first, the intent of the research must be interdisciplinary; second, the questions of values and morals must be raised in their broadest application.

THE SHATTERED SELF

The Psychological and Religious Search for Selfhood

Theodore A. McConnell

A Pilgrim Press Book
Philadelphia

The author wishes to thank the individuals and publishers who have graciously
granted permission to quote from their
copyrighted material. A list of acknowl-
edgments appears on page *xv*. Other brief
quotations are acknowledged in Notes.

Library of Congress Catalog Card Number 75-151893
ISBN 0-8298-0201-0

For Ruth

CONTENTS

INTRODUCTION

Concern with the definition of selfhood in psychology and psychoanalytic thought has pushed the self to the center of interest in the study of man today. Foremost among the disciplines that claim the study of man as their special domain are those of psychology and theology. And it is not accidental that the two disciplines appear to be set upon a collision course toward one another, for each has advanced certain claims and assertions about man that conflict with insights deemed essential by the other. The definition of selfhood is a primary example of disagreement and conflict and the question of selfhood is too critical for us and for these two disciplines to ignore such dissonance. In one form or another the search for an understanding of selfhood underlies much of our contemporary psychological and theological research. From the psychological side the literature concerning selfhood must now be described as a massive and growing body of data and conjectures. From the theological side questions concerning man's religious quest and the interpretation of events of his life continually show the necessity for at least a working concept of the self.

This study examines six basic selfhood models of recent psychology, and then indicates some major areas of relationship and dissonance between these and a variety of theological perspectives. A primary concern of these models is with questions of value or worth. It becomes increasingly apparent with each year that in terms of methodological starting points and the development of models these questions are critical for psychological research. Certainly the same can be said for theology and religious studies. And herein may lie one of the most basic and significant ways to approach the relationship of the two disciplines.

This study has two converging purposes: first, to depict in a concise way the basic models of selfhood in recent psychology; and second, to begin exploring the relationships between these models and some recent theological perspectives of man.

Any attempt to explore the murky areas where psychology and religion interpenetrate must be made with considerable trepidation. The risks of distortion are immense and we lack clear and concrete methods for discerning relationships. We even lack a mutually agreeable and clearly defined vocabulary. Yet it is only by conversation and comparison between different perspectives that we shall ever achieve advances in the understanding of matters of common interest and investigation. The judgment that cross-disciplinary studies are another academic fad belies a superficiality that we cannot afford in contemporary culture. If we are to progress toward a mutuality of insights and discourse, the most expedient method may be through a broad searching of our culture's diverse disciplines at those points where they confront matters of common interest, such as the issues of selfhood, value, and order. A willingness to undertake this kind of comparative task embodies a commitment to seek an enlarged understanding of our culture by focusing upon some basic concepts of its disciplines.

In this instance that task is initiated between two disciplines that share a variety of interests concerned with the definition of selfhood and its values. It is equally important that further studies be undertaken to probe these interests in an utterly open, even a somewhat aggressive manner that seeks to expose the differences and basic disagreements as well as the areas of similarity and "fit." Literature, the arts and the natural sciences all manifest pressing concern with the issues of selfhood and value. Certainly they merit as much attention as I have sought to initiate in this comparative endeavor.

Appreciation is expressed to Dr. Harry C. Meserve, editor of the *Journal of Religion and Health* for permission to use materials in chapters 1 and 2 that were originally published in that journal as part of my papers, "The Course To Adulthood" (No. 5 [3], July 1966) and "Gordon Allport and the Quest for Selfhood" (No. 8 [4], October 1969). I am especially indebted to James Dittes of Yale University for his interest and continuing insights during the past ten years.

ACKNOWLEDGMENTS

Erik H. Erikson:
   Erik H. Erikson, *Identity and the Life Cycle*
Harper & Row, Publishers:
   Abraham Maslow, *Motivation and Personality*
Holt, Rinehart and Winston, Inc.:
   Erich Fromm, *Escape from Freedom*
W. W. Norton & Company, Inc.:
   Erik H. Erikson, *Childhood and Society*
   Erik H. Erikson, *Young Man Luther*
Henry Regnery Company, Publishers:
   Helmut Kuhn, *Encounter with Nothingness*
Yale University Press:
   Gordon W. Allport, *Becoming*
   Paul Tillich, *The Courage to Be*

THE SHATTERED SELF

1

ADULTHOOD and IDENTITY/Erik Erikson

The question of what constitutes adulthood has long plagued all areas of personality studies. What does "adult" mean? What is the course to and within adulthood? How is adulthood to be measured for purposes of diagnosis of the ill and their movement to health? These are all parts of the question of how adulthood is defined.

Although psychologists have always touched on various aspects of adulthood, recent investigations have focused new attention in this area. Erik Erikson's investigations and writings have particular significance because of his concept of identity and its relation to the developing life cycle. Moreover, Erikson's work holds additional interest for theology and religion because he has tried to show how psychological insights relate to religious growth in the biographical study of Luther.*

Erikson isolates the problem of identity as a central characteristic of our time: "The patient of today suffers most under the problem of what he should believe in and who he should—or, indeed, might—be or become; while the patient of early psychoanalysis suffered most under inhibitions which prevented him from being what and who he thought he knew he was." [1] Similarly, other psychologists have drawn attention to the critical need today for illuminating the questions of identity and adulthood. Harry Stack Sullivan's work with the dynamisms and developmental epochs contributed extensively to these matters. Paul Tournier's and Karen Horney's concerns

* For a complete study of Erikson see Robert Coles, *Erik H. Erikson, The Growth of His Work,* Boston, Atlantic-Little, Brown, 1970.

with self-awareness are related to this subject, while Viktor Frankl's logotherapy has been quick to underscore identity and integration as fundamental issues of personality study. Thus from a variety of perspectives, be they social, psychological, or religious, it is not an exaggeration to say that a tremendous need exists for a more precise and comprehensive meaning of "adult."

The breakdowns in society and individuals suggest that we have many persons who are less than healthy or whole. Are these people adults? If so, can we then legitimately distinguish levels of adulthood? Is maturity gained only in some phases of adulthood? Considerable evidence exists to suggest that there are only a few adults in the sense in which Erikson has defined the word. Chronological age may in many respects be the least important or significant factor in defining both adulthood and maturity. A more comprehensive and meaningful way of describing what is meant by an adult is to be found through personality study.

THE DEVELOPMENTAL LIFE CYCLE

In order to understand better what Erikson means by adulthood it is necessary to have some idea of how he has seen the developmental life of the human. In *Childhood and Society* (1950) he suggested that there are eight processes of development on the course to adulthood. These views were refined in a 1959 essay, *Identity and the Life Cycle,* arranging the eight phases or processes in the manner of polar conceptual identities: (1) Trust-Mistrust; (2) Autonomy-Shame and Doubt; (3) Initiative-Guilt;

(4) Industry-Inferiority; (5) Identity-Identity Diffusion;
(6) Intimacy-Self-absorption; (7) Generativity-Stagnation;
(8) Integrity-Despair (and Disgust).

While it has become commonplace to adopt an overall
perspective of the set as a scheme of development, this
can represent less than a full view of the matter. The polar
identities tend to be chronological but there are all sorts
of significant deviations from the linear order. The individual may become blocked at some point and either re-
gress or remain fixated. Or there may be a recapitulation
of earlier phases at some point.

All these possibilities indicate that the person may not
develop through the eight phases. Movement through
them is, of course, necessary for adulthood. But the movement is not mechanical from stage to stage. The process
is dynamic and the effect at each point of the process is
both cumulative and determinative of later developments.
Each phase or stage is characterized by a specific developmental task that has to be solved. The solution is prepared
for in the previous phase and worked out further in later
ones.

It should be noted that the developmental phases are
in no sense identified with age levels of the organism.
Erikson, like Harry Stack Sullivan, Anna Freud, and
Karen Horney, has made a vital contribution to our
understanding here by stressing that maturity or adulthood is seldom achieved by people classed as adults according to the usual social categories. The fifty- or ninety-
year-old person may never have advanced through an
adolescent level. By the same criteria, it is quite possible

for the married eighteen-year-old to be an adult in the full
sense of ego integrity. Erikson's contribution can be seen
by examining his understanding of the eight phases.

(1) *Basic trust-mistrust.* Erikson sees the initial identity crisis of life as one of basic trust versus mistrust.
The attitude of trust is fundamental to all later developments, and corresponds to what Freud called the oral
stage of human development. The sense of trust is an
all-pervasive sort of thing, involving both reliance on
sameness and continuity and a confidence in one's body
and self.

Basic trust or mistrust is established to a considerable
extent, during the first year of life. Its principal source is
the mother or her surrogate. Erikson has demonstrated
the immense influence of the mother in establishing the
pattern of basic trust or mistrust. Her own conditions and
attitudes are really implanted in the infant. The whole
state or quality of relationship between infant and mother
gives a focus to the infant's harmony or disharmony with
self and the world. Basic trust is really "an attitude toward
oneself and the world derived from the experiences of the
first year." [2] Its opposite, mistrust, is characterized by
withdrawal into the self when there is tension with the
self or between the self and others. In this pattern there is
the predisposition for autonomy or shame in the next
developmental phase.

(2) *Autonomy-shame.* The Freudian terminology long
popular for this phase has been the anal mode. The whole
self is here engaged in a battle for autonomy with reten-
tion and elimination as the opposed forces. Shame is basically rage turned against the self. "He who is ashamed

would like to force the world not to look at him, not to notice his exposure. He would like to destroy the eyes of the world. Instead he must wish for his own invisibility." [3]

Shame grows out of mistrust of self and is intensified, reinforced, and expanded by doubt. Many attitudes of later life result from the attainment or non-attainment of autonomy at this stage. Erikson has strongly emphasized the lasting consequences of this result: "From a sense of self-control without loss of self-esteem comes a lasting sense of autonomy and pride; from a sense of muscular and anal impotence, of loss of self-control, and of parental over-control comes a lasting sense of doubt and shame." [4]

(3) *Initiative-guilt.* The foundation for later forms of initiative or guilt stems from early experiences of a sexual nature. Here there is a real danger of developing a sense of guilt for goals desired or acts started. The danger is clear and real, for this phase is especially characterized as a time of genital affection for the mother (on the part of males) or the father (on the part of females) and intense rivalry with that person's adult partner. It is similar to Freud's Oedipus experience. In this phase all the prerequisites for masculine and feminine initiative are present. The consequences of fixation or blockage at this point are the attitudes in later life that one's worth is determined by what one does or is going to do rather than by what one is as a person. [5]

(4) *Industry-inferiority.* The initiative pattern is usually worked out or implemented in terms of securing recognition by making things. What Erikson depicted as the industry-inferiority crisis is an experimental discrimination between work and play. In the play world the child

is seen to learn either mastery or to fail in gaining this mastery. Here is the foundation for handling conflicts. We are confronted here with the developing sense of an ability to make things and make them well or a sense of inadequacy and inferiority.[6] This phase is comparable to Freud's latency stage.

(5) *Identity-identity diffusion.* This phase becomes critical in adolescence and is the time of the greatest frequency of arrested development. Here tremendous physiological and social forces are brought to bear upon the individual to accomplish some form of self-integration. But to gain self-identity is not possible without previous basic trust and a promise or high expectation of individual fulfillment. This synthesis or establishing of identity is "more than the sum of childhood identifications. It is the inner capital accrued from all those experiences of each successive stage, when successful identification led to a successful alignment of the individual's basic drives with his endowment and his opportunities."[7] Probably the most troublesome area at this time is the adolescent's inability to find a clear occupational decision.

(6) *Intimacy-self-absorption.* The intimacy crisis really borders on the preadult level in many respects. Some firm sense of identity must precede the intimacy crisis. If there is a latent weakness in identity then a breakdown appears at the time of attempted intimacy, whereas the achievement of intimacy carries one into adulthood.

By intimacy Erikson does not refer entirely to sexual relationships. Rather it includes the whole field of sensitivity in interpersonal relations and the ability to accomplish depth in friendships involving mutual sharing and

bearing of burdens. Its opposite is self-absorption or dis-
tantiation, which is the "readiness to repudiate, to isolate,
and destroy those forces and persons who appear as dan-
gerous to the self." [8] When intimacy is not achieved there
is, on the one hand, isolation of the self characterized by
a pattern of highly formal interpersonal relations, and on
the other hand, repeated attempts and failures at intimacy.

Although intimacy involves an infinite complex of emotions and relations in addition to the sexual, the successful
completion of the phase is impossible unless a pattern of
heterosexual relations is established. Genitality is a significant aspect of the whole intimacy complex and is not
to be treated lightly. Genitality is not the mere attainment
of orgasm but a genital sensitivity involving discharge of
bodily tensions.[9] Erikson has pointed out why the estab-
lishment of regular heterosexual relationships is vitally
important for human development and health: "The experience of climactic mutuality or orgasm provides a su-
preme example of the mutual regulation of complicated
patterns and in some ways appeases the potential rages
caused by the daily evidence of the oppositeness of male
and female, of fact and fancy, of love and hate, of work
and play." [10]

It is in the reduction of the rage established by the
oppositeness of the sexes and their life patterns and relationships that the course toward adulthood and maturity
is advanced. For Erikson it is not possible to advance
into adulthood without a satisfactory resolution of this
phase. Which is to say that Erikson is very definite about
the necessity of a full marital, sexual relationship for ad-
vancement into adult selfhood. This is the natural order

of the human animal and it cannot be ignored or de-emphasized in thinking about a psychological definition of the self. Because marriage provides the opportunities for a complete experience of the regulation of man's complicated emotional and psychological patterns of living, including his sexuality, it is a condition of the movement toward adult selfhood.

This definition poses problems for the single, the celebate, and the homosexual. Simply put, they have not attained adult selfhood. It is important to face this situation squarely and not attempt to redefine or qualify Erikson's model. The unmarried person has not attained adult selfhood on Erikson's terms. Marriage here means heterosexual union and cohabitation.*

* Generally speaking, religious and theological thinking has not made marriage a condition of adult selfhood. While not disapproving marriage as such, Paul clearly stated that the unmarried state was preferable, given the condition of the world and the total life of man (1 Cor. 7: 8; 25-28; 38). Similarly, Augustine and Aquinas were inclined positively toward the single state. Recent theologians have expressed a variety of opinions but nowhere is it possible to find an absolute requirement of heterosexual marriage as a necessary condition of adult selfhood. One of the most complete and useful recent discussions of marriage, sexuality, and selfhood in a Christian context is that of Anglican theologian Norman Pittenger's *Making Sexuality Human,* 1970, Philadelphia, The Pilgrim Press. Pittenger fully depicts the basic views of marriage and sexuality in Christian theology, analyzes the implications for the single person, and provides the basis for a comparison of Christian and psychological views of the matter.

(7) *Generativity-stagnation.* Experience in sexual relations and other levels of intimacy does not conclude human development. What Erikson calls generativity advances the person into adulthood and toward maturity. Generativity goes deeply into the experience of marriage in which there is authentic mutuality. For it is the "wish to combine personalities and energies in the production and care of common offspring." [11] Generativity is not to be confused with the mere wish to have children. It involves both a sense of common concern for the race and a love of self and mate sufficient to produce the desire to perpetuate these personalities.

Where true generativity fails to be achieved, physiological and emotional stagnation occurs. There is an immense development of pseudo-intimate relations in this arrested state. One might add that it is highly prevalent and often the seat not only of disturbed marital relations but also of problems in child rearing.

(8) *Integrity-despair.* The final or most accomplished phase of adulthood is the achievement of ego or self-integrity. Maturity is distinguished by the following achievements: performing the function of taking care of things and persons; adapting to the triumphs and disappointments involved in the structure of being; acting as the originator of other persons; being the generator of things and ideas. [12]

Integrity is in a sense a lifelong process. And yet Erikson wants to make it clear that a level of integrity and the integration of personality components is possible early in life, provided the proper conditions have been fulfilled. While ego integrity involves some imprecise or as yet undefined elements, several of the more explicit attributes are as follows. The person who has accomplished ego integrity or maturity is characterized by his acceptance of his own life cycle as a unique event and the only one possible for him. There is a new, different love of one's parents that is free from the wish for them to be different. There is a full acceptance of the fact that one's life is one's responsibility alone. The mature person has achieved some sense of comradeship with historical persons who are worthy models for dignity and love. There is a readiness to defend one's life style against both physical and economic threats. Finally, the mature person is characterized by an emotional integration of such a sort that one can participate by following and also recognize and accept responsibility for leadership when it seems appropriate.

ADULTHOOD AND THE MATURE ADULT

The view that Erikson has advanced of adulthood and of its maturity places primary emphasis upon identity formation. Adulthood has stages of growth within itself. Similarly, if the identity crisis is not solved, one remains in some phase of adolescence. Erikson's work suggests that many people who are regarded by society as adults are actually still in an adolescent phase of development. By supplying new meaning for adult and maturity he has given us more precise tools of discrimination.

Many of the attributes of personality that become sources of adult tensions and disputes are characteristic of the patterns of adolescence. The choice of negative identity, the inability to experience intimate relationships, the injury of other persons through patterns of ambivalence and narcissism, the inability to concentrate on required tasks, and a self-destructive preoccupation with onesided activities may all be indicative of either arrested development or regression to an adolescent state based upon an unsatisfactory solution of the identity crisis.

The essential data we have to deal with in the course to adulthood and on to its maturity are, as Erikson has made clear, the primal origins of the person and how fully his identity has been established. Erikson has depicted the basic crippling emotional and psychological forces that impair and block the road to maturity. As a result of them, where there is no distinct identity that is accepted and knows what it stands for, there is no maturity of life.

ADULTHOOD AND DEVELOPMENT IN RELIGION

In considering Erikson's definition of adulthood we must ask what implications it holds for religion. What is the relationship of this model to the types of maturity that theology has held necessary for a religious view of man? In seeking to answer these kinds of questions Erikson's work can be of particular value in itself. For unlike many investigators in psychology, Erikson has contributed significant material analyzing the relationships of psychology and religious growth. His outstanding study of Luther's development focuses attention on these relationships. Having drawn a comprehensive picture of the development of the life cycle, Erikson has built on this in his study of Luther and demonstrated in a fascinating way the parallels and relationships of influence between personality and religious development.

(1) *Age and adulthood*. One vital implication of Erikson's definition of adult is that religion can be freed of the social myth of adulthood defined according to chronological age. In greater or less degree it would seem that only a few persons could be said to be adults in the full sense of Erikson's terms.

Religion has tended to see adulthood as a state characterized by a degree of self-love that frees the person from continuous concern for his being and enhances his status before society. This self-love is seen as derived from divine love and as necessary in order to experience divine and human love.

Some interpreters of religion have asserted that only the person who is free of self-hate is capable of love for others and God.[13] This is said to be a basic characteristic of maturity in the adulthood of faith. It is paralleled by what Erikson described in the identity and integrity crises. Paul Tillich, a significant representative of this kind of religious thinking, defined maturity in these terms: "By affirming our being we participate in the self-affirmation of being-itself." [14]

Erikson found in Luther's life data for asserting that there is an adulthood and a maturity in religion somewhat parallel to development in the human life cycle. Struggle is basic to the forms of growth that are wholly intertwined in the religious man. There is a progression from seeing

God in the role of a dreaded and untrustworthy father to experiencing him as the companion who is also one's lord. It is the movement from God the enemy to God the friend, as Tillich expressed it.[15] The development is similar to that experienced in the life cycle with respect to one's parents. With movement into integrity there is growth and change in how one sees one's parents. They are no longer objects of fear, distrust, or the wish to alter their nature. Erikson has suggested that here as elsewhere the natural development is a pattern or clue showing the parallel shape of religious growth in the experience of God.

(2) *An image of man.* Similarly, Erikson has found considerable affinity between his view of man and the religious view of man proposed by Luther. Luther, like contemporary identity psychologists, called for a redefinition of man. The product of such redefinition is, in each case, born out of struggle and reorganization of the personality and its life pattern. It involves struggle, crisis, hopelessness, despair, and a recovery from repeated crises. Adulthood is a difficult attainment when it is seen in a psychological perspective and model such as that proposed by Erikson. The achievement demanded for the phases of identity in his model has certain parallels in the demands for achievement of a religious model such as that suggested by Luther.

Looking toward maturity or meaning in both personal and religious growth is "to be at one with an ideology in the process of rejuvenation; it implies a successful sublimation of one's libidinal strivings, and it manifests itself

in a liberated craftsmanship." [16] Erikson finds in Luther
a "new emphasis on man in inner conflict and his salvation through introspective perfection." [17] This is the solving of the identity problem and movement toward integrity. And Erikson is quite willing to see that this can be
accomplished through religious development. Religion can
be a plausible pattern within which to work through the
life cycle problems to adulthood and maturity. There is
a kind of verification of identity through a combination
of work and love.[18]

(3) *Maturity and adulthood.* Erikson has attempted
to outline the significant differences between a religious
quest for adulthood and ordinary development. While the
integrity crisis comes last in the ordinary human life cycle,
he found that a theology such as Luther's advocates a
vitally different pattern. In this different pattern the integrity crisis is lifelong and chronic.[19] This is the point of
potential growth in a dimension not found in other life
cycles. For the religious man "can permit himself to face
as permanent the trust problem which drives others in
whom it remains or becomes dominant into denial, despair, and psychosis. He acts as if mankind were starting
all over with his own beginning as an individual, conscious
of his singularity as well as his humanity." [20]

The ability to live with and face as a permanent factor
in one's life the whole problem of trust is basic to a religious maturity. In this way the man of faith works intensively throughout his life with the problems of identity
and integrity. As such he is to be differentiated from the

bulk of humanity in terms of the potential source of personal and social creativity.

The most common objection raised in psychology about religion is that theology and faith foster a kind of regression in personality development. Erikson has contended that while religious development is certainly parallel to regression, this is only the case in a particular sense. In fact, religious maturity is only seemingly and not actually regressive. Of course, immature forms of religious behavior are regressive but in mature religion Erikson found that the return to infantile trust patterns was specifically for the purpose of healing the sick or immature self.

What Erikson and others are suggesting at this point is that there are usually two kinds of religion—mature and immature. It is true that much behavior frequently considered religious is regressive. But this kind of religion is not a mature or authentic kind of religion. The movement to religious adulthood is something different and must not be mistaken for the usual forms. Regression in the course to religious maturity is seen by Erikson as fostering a creative recovery: "At their creative best, religions retrace our earliest inner experiences. At the same time they keep alive the common symbols of integrity distilled by the generations." [21]

The historical consciousness and emphasis on religious maturity found in theologies like those of Paul Tillich (*The Courage to Be*), Reinhold Niebuhr (*The Nature and Destiny of Man*), and Richard Rubenstein (*After Auschwitz* and *The Religious Imagination*) is basic to

integration for it establishes a sense of comradeship with
people of the past who have contributed to the creative
and generative forces of life. This kind of emphasis also
utilizes the forces that previous generations have success-
fully used in the task of integration. The sought-for faith
goes back to restoring the basic trust of infancy. As such
it is taken as God's plan and form of living for mankind.

Many theologians have claimed that there is a resolution of the identity problem in the discovery of the God
who is said to be Lord. Paul Tillich struggled to express
this often misunderstood argument by writing: "One can
become aware of the God above the God of theism in the
anxiety of guilt and condemnation when the traditional
symbols that enable man to withstand the anxiety of guilt
and condemnation have lost their power." [22]

Reference to Tillich's theology in this case is of particular relevance, for Erikson sought to enjoin the psychoanalytic debate with religion in terms of Tillich's definition
of religion as ultimate concern. It is with respect to this
definition of religion that psychoanalysis offers us an
enlarged vision of the self as identified or whole. In its
roots and essence psychoanalysis aims to free people for
ultimate concerns, including those of the religious quest.
But there is a critical priority or ordering process in pur-
suing this quest and its implicit search for identity. That
is to say, only the relatively free person (in terms of self-
image and identity) can follow the religious quest without
distorting or perverting it. Ultimate concerns "can begin
to be ultimate only in those rare moments and places
where neurotic resentments end and where mere readjust-

ment is transcended." [23] This is to say, finally, that the religious quest for the ultimate is well advised to establish its roots in an awareness of the self that has mastered resentment, hostility, hate, and destructiveness through the discovery of identity.

2

The AUTONOMOUS SELF/Gordon Allport

Among the growing body of literature about selfhood and identity the writings of the late Gordon Allport provide a set of notable definitions that are especially relevant to the relationships of psychology and religion. While Allport's perspective is distinctive in several ways, probably his best known and most important contribution is that of a methodological contrast between what he called the Lockean and Leibnizian traditions. The Lockean (for John Locke) is characterized by seeing the mind as essentially passive while the Leibnizian (after Leibniz) regards it as active or dynamic.[1] This contrast is paralleled by one in the study of religious behavior and experience, that of extrinsic and intrinsic religion.

THE DEFINITION OF RELIGION

If the definition of religion is to encompass the empirical differences exhibited in society, Allport asserted that it would need to embody a distinction that not only allows for these differences but attempts to evaluate them. Definitions like that of religion as "escape from reality" fail to contribute anything substantive to the discussion because all methodologies tend to see reality through the phenomena from which they spring. Moreover, it will not suffice to define religion as a replication of culture for we can readily isolate persons and behavior identified with religious enterprises that do not mirror cultural belief.[2] We must therefore recognize a plurality of religious experiences that we can then specify by quality and personality traits. In his studies on personality and prejudice Allport suggested that there are two qualities of religious behavior that are broadly applicable to the study of religions.

Extrinsic or immature religion tends to be identified with minimal involvement of the self, with rigidity of doctrinal beliefs, with socially conservative or constrictive views and a high degree of inability to tolerate ambiguity in beliefs and practices. Extrinsic religion is a habit or device used by persons to achieve certain objectives or to satisfy certain needs but it is not something that is lived. Allport incisively provided the complementary theological and psychological descriptions of extrinsic religion: "In theological terms the extrinsically religious person turns to God, but does not turn away from self. For this reason, his religion is primarily a shield for self-centeredness." "In motivational terms, the extrinsic religious sentiment is not a driving or integral motive. It serves other motives: the need for security, the need for status, the need for self-esteem. In terms of developmental psychology, the formation is immature." [3]

By contrast, intrinsic or mature religion is characterized by intensive involvement and self-commitment, a flexible and liberal social outlook and an ability to tolerate and effectively utilize the ambiguity present in human life. Moreover, the intrinsic religious person displays a functional autonomy and integration of selfhood that imparts the so-called transforming power to religious practice.

Intrinsic or mature religion is: (1) well differentiated; (2) dynamic in character in spite of its derivative nature; (3) productive of a consistent morality; (4) comprehensive; (5) integral; and (6) fundamentally heuristic. In essence, these are the application to religion of basic personality measurements of maturity. They include a widened range of interest, insight into the self and development of a comprehensive philosophy of life.[4]

Selfhood or maturity in religion is identified with the psychological concepts of selfhood defined in personality studies. The two experiences are congruent as they endeavor to define behavior characteristics in human life. From the standpoint of religion, another way of explicating this definition is in terms of the distinctions between belief and doubt.

BELIEF AND DOUBT

Allport applied his extrinsic-intrinsic model to the central dichotomy of religious experience, that of belief and doubt. In this instance we are asked to consider the presence of two kinds of belief and doubt in shaping religious identity. Heuristic belief, a belief that is held tentatively or modified in the light of a more valid belief, corresponds to intrinsic religion. Intrinsic or mature religion, characterized by heuristic belief, argues for the necessity of doubt as part of the religious experience.

As in his other definitions, Allport distinguished two types or models when defining doubt. There is a kind of absolutist, scientific doubting that shares affinities with extrinsic or immature religion: it fails to recognize the limitations of its methodology, dogmatically defends its axioms and propositions and displays a high degree of inability to tolerate ambiguity. In contrast to this kind of doubting there is the doubting that is an integral part of heuristic belief. It is the consistent attitude of openness, flexibility, and tentativeness toward belief—an attitude of willingness to re-examine and alter belief in the light of new evidence.

The clash of scientific, extrinsic doubting and heuristic belief presents three alternative possibilities: (1) the absolute triumph of scientific doubt—itself impervious to doubt and thus a fundamental contradiction; (2) a schizophrenia whereby both scientific doubting and heuristic belief are employed in different segments of human life without being related; and (3) "a ceaseless struggle to assimilate the scientific frame of thought within an expanded religious frame." [5]

The third alternative was obviously Allport's choice. It opts for the toleration of ambiguity and the attempt at a more rational and integrated use of doubt in shaping the self. Belief is a component of selfhood resting upon probabilities reinforced by sense perception and reason. Should these reinforcements be lacking, belief becomes delusion just as it is often said to be knowledge when the reinforcements constitute a maximum degree of accord. But belief remains based on probabilities and thus it is open to modification by subsequent experience. A chief element in this experience is the complex development of personality.

PERSONALITY

For Allport personality was an all-inclusive concept for describing man. Personality is more inclusive than the self or the realm of consciousness. It is the dynamic organization of that complex of mutually interacting elements generally named mind and body that result in man's behavior and thought patterns. An awareness of the nature and complexity of personality more clearly enables us to understand the self and its functional role in human life.

One of Allport's most well-known concepts for depicting the nature and functions of personality is that of functional autonomy. Functional autonomy is a way of seeing human motivation as part of personality while maintaining that all aspects of personality are not aspects of motivation. Human motives are varied, dynamic and growing systems that are functionally independent or autonomous of their origins. Obviously a functionally autonomous view of motivation rejects any idea of static energies or systems. In contrast, it sees all aspects of personality as phenomena of transformation. Functional autonomy does not refer to certain basic bodily motivations such as drives, reflex actions, primary reinforcements, habits, etc. that have been demonstrated to be functionally allied with their origins. Functional autonomy refers to other equally vital but more broadly pervasive aspects of motivation such as principles of organizing energy levels, principles of mastery and competence and principles of propriate patterning. These principles are said to be functionally independent or autonomous of their origins as they operate in personality development and maintenance. "Taken together [these principles] amount to saying that functional autonomy comes about because it is the essence or care of the purposive nature of man." [6]

According to Allport a functionally autonomous perspective of motivation allows us to make certain necessary adjustments in the concept of self as it has been depicted

in much psychology and philosophy. The self is seen as
a dynamic aspect of the more inclusive concept, personality, but selfhood is not a factotum. Motives are accorded
an autonomy from their origins in the functioning of
personality. And thus a critical danger in definitions of
selfhood—overstressing the function of consciousness—is
avoided. The self involves functionally autonomous elements and this demands us to recognize that "however
transient the consciousness of self may be, all sensing,
acting and willing are, at bottom, owned and that selfhood is the central presupposition we must hold in examining the psychological states of human beings." [7]

In the search for models for selfhood one of the most
vexing dilemmas of personality investigations is that of
growth or maturity in selfhood. While there has come
to be a broad area of agreement about the necessity for
some balance between individual growth and cohesion
with society, there is little agreement about the characteristics of balance. In this dilemma Allport was emphatic
in his attempt to refute any crude or simplistic concept
of balance or equilibrium. The error of such simplistic
concepts is their non-empirical basis. Are such concepts
as balance, equilibrium, and tension reduction authentically human or realistic when they are proposed as models
for personality? Perhaps "whatever our definition of nor-
mality turns out to be it must allow for serviceable imbal-
ances within personality and between person and society." [8]

Man is not so much in equilibrium as restless. Therefore personality study must seek a broader understanding
of selfhood and personality than that of balance. Allport

proposed that personality be seen as a functioning system, an incomplete system, but one embodying diverse elements in mutual interaction. Within this system there is what might be called the proprium or self. The proprium includes a sense of bodily self, a sense of continuing self-identity, self-esteem and pride, extension of the self, the self-image, the self as rational striver and problem solver.[9] The self is thereby defined as more than self-image. It is a system within personality and it is possibly the most significant system for comprehending and unifying personality.

Fundamentally three traits summarize Allport's concept of the self: (1) the expanding self; (2) detachment and insight or self-objectification; (3) integration or self-unification. At various times these have been expanded to six traits of maturity or growth: expansion of the sense of self; warm relating of self to others; emotional security or self-acceptance; realistic perception, skills and assignments; self-objectification, combining insights and humor; and a unifying philosophy of life. The expanding self describes the collected variety of interests, values, and beliefs that come to be specified in individual human life. The self or mature personality displays a willingness and flexibility to expand this collection and assimilate its variety throughout the life cycle.

In displaying expansion and assimilation the mature self exhibits an ability to be reflective and insightful about its collection of interests, values, and traits. There is a quality of objectification about oneself (detachment and insight). Finally, the mature self displays a unifying philosophy of life by which the variety of interests and traits are integrated and assimilated within a context of tolerance for ambiguity. By contrast, the immature self and the immature religion lack these distinctive developmental characteristics.

The three characteristics provide a composite view of the self in psychology and religion. The view is not that of a developmental sequence but of a continuing assimilation of complementary and interacting characteristics, a process Allport called becoming. The self as becoming is characterized by a "disposition to realize its possibilities, i.e., to become characteristically human at all stages of development." Fundamental to this process is individuation, the composite of an expanding self that displays detachment, insight, and integration. Individuation is "the formation of an individual style of life that is self-aware, self-critical and self-enhancing." [10] Through the process of organizing interests and impulses into a pattern or reasonable organization (becoming), the individual or self is formed. Seen in its largest and final context this process is intent upon relating the self to the totality of human life and reality. It is in this task that Allport found a significant role for intrinsic religion and heuristic belief as providing a perspective and evaluation of human life.

Allport regarded intrinsic religion and psychology as similar in their demands for order and integration in personality. In satisfying the demands of this quest intrinsic religion offers a unique experience. It is said to be that "portion of personality that arises at the core of life and is directed toward the infinite. It is the region of mental

life that has the longest-range intentions, and for this reason is capable of conferring marked integration upon personality." [11] The religious quest for selfhood embodies
a striving to enlarge the self, placing it within an ultimate
context whereby its limitations are recognized and affirmed together with an expanding integration of its potential for development and change. This perspective of
human life is intent upon integrating the psychological
and religious quests for selfhood.

THE QUEST FOR SELFHOOD

Allport's concern for defining the self in psychology and
religion is comparable to a similar interest in such otherwise diverse psychological perspectives as those of Erik
Erikson, Harry Stack Sullivan, Eric Fromm, Carl Rogers,
Earl Loomis, and Elihu Howland. While certain parallels
in thought can be observed in these diverse materials
(especially in terms of the ideas of identity, integration,
individuation, and becoming), Allport's perspective is
marked by a concern with the relationship of psychology
and religion. In particular his development of the two
types of religion and their expression in the dynamics of
personality is significant. While Allport found major dissonance between the data of psychological and religious
behavior in many sectors of human life (such as prejudice), in the study of selfhood he was increasingly concerned with a convergence of perspectives. But for the
convergence to be valid he had to distinguish in a consistent manner between types of religion and types of
personality. Thus intrinsic religious behavior is seen as

complementary to and often associated with the mature or integrated self. In fact some of the distinguishing characteristics of intrinsic religious behavior (ability to tolerate ambiguity, flexibility of doctrinal perspective, social concern and elasticity of outlook) are linked to mature and integrated self-awareness and objectification.

It is significant to note that a similar distinction can be found in certain kinds of modern theology. Such otherwise diverse perspectives as those of Paul Tillich, Karl Barth, Dietrich Bonhoeffer, and the Niebuhr brothers rely upon two types of religious behavior in developing theological insight. For Tillich, the distinction was that of ultimate concern and faith, of heteronomy and theonomy, or of agape and morality; for Barth, of revelation or the "Word of God" and natural religion; for Bonhoeffer, of religion and religionless Christianity; for Reinhold Niebuhr, of social and moral truth versus institutional religious practices and allegiances; and for H. Richard Niebuhr, the responsible self and rigid doctrinal allegiances. While this comparison is in no way meant to suggest a similarity of outlook or concern in these theologies, it does point to the one rather irreducible methodological similarity of relying upon two types of religion and the implicit value judgments concerning them. Allport's psychology stands as a contemporary schema that has clarified this distinction in the quest for selfhood. The significance of its implication for the relationship of psychological and religious perspectives can hardly be overestimated. It has demonstrated the futility of attempting to reduce religious or psychological behavior to a single, solitary set of relationships.

At the same time caution should be exercised by pointing out that the perspective is limited by its relative lack of attention to the influence and conditioning of society upon selfhood and belief. Allport's emphasis tended to concentrate upon individual psychology and the relationship to belief. But the linkage of personality characteristics and kinds of religious behavior and belief represents only one dimension in the process of self-formation.

Ultimately Allport's definition of religion may involve as many significant implications for theological method as it does for the psychological study of religion and religious experience. In any event his clarification of the phenomenon of two types of religion and the relationships of these to personality provides a set of methodological tools that substantially advances the discussion about the nature of selfhood. Moreover, his perspective marks another significant development in its identification and description of the potentialities in a religious perspective of the self's relation to human life or the totality of being. Consistent with his methodology and outlook, Allport regarded this as the attempt to enlarge and complete the self-image by placing it in a larger context. In this new context the self's limitations as well as its potentialities were affirmed and its ability to tolerate and utilize the ambiguities of human life becomes a way of seeking truth and a more humane existence.

Allport's writing was consistently infused with the sense of the individual's importance. His model for selfhood was forged patiently under the hammer of truth and empirical reality, tempered by what he called the need for humility. Humility in investigation and discourse was a virtue he

found appropriate for psychology. He envisioned that
humility as a compound of patience, tentativeness, and
realism in the light of empirical data. Consistently critical
of mechanistic interpretations of man, shortly before his
death Allport summarized the quest for an enlarged psychology of man: "What then is my personal idea? I sup-
pose it has to do with the search for a theoretical system
—for one that will allow for truth wherever found, one
that will encompass the totality of human experience and
do full justice to the nature of man." [12] In the final analysis such a model merits the most exacting pursuit and
admiration that psychology and religion can offer.

3

The SOCIAL ROOTS of SELFHOOD/Erich Fromm

In a wide variety of writings Erich Fromm has developed
a distinctive concept of the self emphasizing the social
forces of human development. Fromm has been especially
interested in developing this model in terms of contrasting
traits such as those of flexibility and inflexibility, aloneness
and relationship, and the normal and neurotic.

FLEXIBILITY-INFLEXIBILITY

For Fromm two primary groupings of traits can be observed in persons. The inflexible traits are basic to all
persons and remain relatively constant: hunger, thirst, the
need for sleep and self-preservation. The flexible traits
may be present in greater or less degree in the developing
self: love, destructiveness, sadism, the tendency to submit,
lust for power, detachment, desire for self-aggrandizement,
passion for thirst, enjoyment of sensual pleasure and fear
of sensuality.[1] These traits are accompanied by the syndromes of growth and decay. Decay involves love of death
whereas growth involves love of life, love of man, and
independence.[2] Both syndromes are contagious and thus
the self acquires an affinity for one or the other through
environmental associations, particularly those of the
family.

Behind Fromm's emphasis on decay and death lies his
judgment that maternal ties precede those of Freud's
Oedipus relationship. In love, fear, and hatred the self is
said to be more consumed with the wish for maternal love
and fear of her destructiveness than anything else. The result is conflict between the tendency to remain tied to the
mother and the impulse to be born, to grow, to progress.

The mature or healthy self chooses growth and progression to the eventual exclusion of fragmentation and decay.[3]

ALONENESS AND RELATIONSHIP

The primary physiological traits represented by the flexible and inflexible are not the only needs of the self. Alongside these are the more subtle and equally compelling
needs to be related to the world outside the self and to
avoid aloneness. Thus the self also can be characterized
by the relationships that give man security and a feeling
of well-being. But there is a delicate balance between too
much relationship with others (being dependent upon
them) and too little relationship (feeling isolated and
alone). Development of a balance between these two ex-
tremes is likely to be a tense experience, but it is abso-
lutely necessary for growth into adult selfhood.

For Fromm the developing self attains a degree of
maturity or realization in affirming its social roots. Persons
develop and grow in communities and their self-image is
inevitably influenced and shaped by those communities.
"There is only one possible, productive solution for the
relationship of individualized man with the world: his active solidarity with all men and his spontaneous activity,
love and work which unite him again with the world,
not by primary ties but as a free and independent individual." [4]

NORMAL AND NEUROTIC

According to Fromm understanding the self is something
that often becomes tied up in the dilemma of defining

normalcy and health. Normal or healthy can be defined from the standpoint of society or the individual. And herein lies a conflict; for social and individual goals are not always identical. Social definitions of normal usually emphasize the role of the self within society whereas individuals usually seek a maximum of growth and happiness, irrespective of social role functions. But the socially normal person may surrender essential elements of selfhood in order to fulfill a particular role in society. In these instances we are confronted with the possibility that the normal person may be less healthy in terms of human values than the neurotic.[5]

The dilemma involving conflict over normal and neurotic patterns points to one of Fromm's basic convictions concerning the self—the importance of choice and self-determination. To be human is to be confronted with the necessity of making choices about the course of the self. In so doing the self is conditioned by the society but it must not escape from its individuality by relying upon social salvation. Wrong choices inevitably render the self incapable of salvation. The search for truth or salvation is therefore directly related to the attainment of freedom and independence of the self. This model of selfhood shows the aims of human life to be independence, integrity, and ability to love.[6]

SOCIAL SELFHOOD

In tracing the social roots of selfhood Fromm found society simultaneously encouraging greater self-independence and greater isolation and aloneness. The result is that human relationships have increasingly assumed the nature of manipulation as contrasted to direct and open human relatedness and friendship. Moreover, this trait of manipulation has come to characterize much of man's relatedness to himself. The social conditioning of self-development has resulted in a new self-image. Man sees himself as a commodity.[7]

The loss of the self is directly related to a misuse of the total social roots of selfhood. When role expectations of society are allowed to impress themselves uncritically upon the self, greater isolation, aloneness and loss of the self are apparent. But the corrective is also to be found in the social roots of the self. It is to be found in those roots where man is productively related to the world and is able to respond to it authentically. "The problem of each individual is precisely that of the level of freedom he has reached. The fully awakened, productive man is a free man because he can live authentically—his own self being the source of his life." [8]

THE STRUGGLE WITH AUTHORITY

Freedom of the self introduces Fromm's final category for describing the self—that of the struggle with authority. Authoritarian thinking is characterized by the conviction that the self is determined by forces outside itself and the only possible course of action lies in submission to these forces. The three principal forces of submission or "escape" are simple submission to the authority, destruction of self or the authority and conformity to authoritarian standards.

In contrast to authoritarian thinking the self can realize a positive freedom. Positive freedom "implies the principle that there is no higher power than this unique individual self, that man is the center and purpose of his life; that the growth and realization of man's individuality is an end that can never be subordinated to purposes which are supposed to have greater dignity." [9] This freedom is always limited by the real possibilities of human life. It consists in choosing between these real possibilities based upon an awareness of the alternatives and their consequences. At their best these real possibilities or aims of human life (independence, integrity, the ability to love) allow for the self to surmount the struggle with authority, achieving a liberation and identity. Love defined as capacity for concern, responsibility and respect of persons, together with an authentic desire for their growth, is the consistent characteristic of human identity. Love defined in this way is a social attribute that points to the self as innately social in its development and identity.

FROMM'S MODEL

Fromm's semi-popular writings are imbued with assumptions common to a wide range of existential thought. The concern with aloneness, the necessity for individual choices in the present, the reliance upon self-determination, the quest for authentic existence and freedom for the self are to be found in such otherwise different philosophers and theologians as Albert Camus, Jean Paul Sartre, Gabriel Marcel, Martin Buber, Rudolf Bultmann, and Paul Tillich. Indeed this gathering of selfhood traits has emerged as one of the distinctive marks of the existential movements in this age. Fromm has endorsed this credo as the authentic reading of the age and its people. He has directed attention to the manipulation of the self by society as well as by itself and has especially been concerned with the manipulative force of social evil. In recent theology Reinhold Niebuhr has devoted a lifetime of work to exposing and confronting the issues of social evil. Other recent theologies have shared a similar concern, most notably those of Paul Tillich, Emil Brunner, and William Temple.

Fromm's emphasis of the loss of selfhood and identity as a result of the forces and pressures of modern urban technological society is a theme that has been widely accepted in recent religious thought. Helmut Kuhn summarized it in 1949:

A man working on an assembly line, making he knows not what for he knows not whom, nor caring in the least, next to his elbow a fellow worker whom he does not know (tomorrow it will be someone else), earning just enough to enable him to rise in the morning to return to his place on the assembly line, enough also to make him shoulder, hour by hour, all the empty time that is still ahead of him, and to throw away as much of this burden as he can upon unenjoyable pleasures. . . . This is the unadorned void. The guilt void meanwhile haunts the luxurious office, the suburban mansion, the opera house where a singer sells his voice at so high a price that he can afford to forget about that which is priceless in music.[10]

Recent theological responses to this human plight have tended to parallel Fromm's in arguing that the corrective is to be found in a social context also. The answer is said to be in a rediscovery of the self's social roots whereby man is productively related to the world and is able to live in it with some measure of well-being and satisfaction. Reinhold Niebuhr has spoken of the vital importance of the communities of family, tribe, nation, and culture for self-realization and the attainment of well-being.[11] His brother, the late H. Richard Niebuhr, demonstrated how the church is a community pointing man to the realization of an ethical life of responsible selfhood.[12] James M. Gustafson has shown how the church is a multi-dimensional human community (i.e., natural, political, linguistic, interpretative, historical, believing, and action oriented) that provides man a basis for self-discovery, self-realization, and making ethical decisions.[13] Waldo Beach has pointed to the significance of the communities of government, law, and the universities as sources for man's future development and well-being.[14] Julian Hartt and Rubem Alves have depicted the critical role of political communities and cultural heritages in the development and liberation of the self.[15] Finally, Pierre Teilhard de Chardin took the matter even further by suggesting that the self must be related consciously to the total universe and all of nature. Human development, including personality development, is an emergent, evolving process intimately linked to the ever-expanding development of the universe of which man is a small part. Man's future survival is said to be in a closer identification and harmony with this unfolding process.[16]

Interestingly, Fromm and many theologians also have shared a concern with the self's quest for truth and salvation (or self-authentication, self-validation, authentic existence) as the basic answer to society's dilemma of evil. But beyond this there is a rather sharp difference. Fromm affirms the innate integrity and self-sufficiency of the self—if not realized at least in potential. There is no higher power than the self. All matters of self-determination and truth are attainable by the self—a viewpoint similar to Camus and perhaps even more to Jean Paul Sartre but certainly not to most theologians. The divergence of perspective makes clearer a significant point of contrast between many of the recent selfhood models of psychology and religion: a use of similar terms without common meanings. Social evil, freedom, salvation, choice and truth as defined and used in a variety of ways by the psychologists are not identical or even similar to theological usages of these terms. Superficial similarities or even certain conceptual agreements (e.g., the impact of aloneness and alienation, the pervasive force of social evil, manipulation of the self) must not be allowed to mask essential differences and basic conflicts. Fromm's image of man is such a point. It challenges the theological images of man even as these confront Fromm's model. Unfortunately neither side has argued the issues to any significant degree. In *The Plague, The Stranger,* and *The Myth of Sisyphus* Albert Camus pressed the issues to a greater extent than either the psychologists or the theologians have done. More often than not the psychologists and theologians have tended to incorporate selected parts of Camus for support, while refusing to confront their models with his.

Fromm's eclectic psychology presupposes Freudian analysis in depicting human development but he alters the theory at critical points (such as the Oedipus relationship, the social roots of alienation, the solving of authority and autonomy relationships). His early work served a useful function in pointing to the social dimensions of selfhood and the problems of alienation in contemporary culture. However, Fromm has attempted to expand the analysis into a complete theory of man without adequately seeing the limitations of such an enterprise. The social model for selfhood is inevitably limited in perspective if it is not liberally tempered by the organic and psychological data of man's life cycle. Moreover, any scientific theory must give some systematic generalizations that are capable of being empirically tested. It will not do simply to make an assertion or claim if we are to know anything with certainty. And it is this data that receives such scant attention from Fromm. The result is a collection of sweeping generalizations and value judgments whose validity is never firmly established.

4

The QUEST for MEANING/Viktor Frankl

Among contemporary psychological models for selfhood Viktor Frankl's is one of the most metaphysical and speculative. Frankl's concept of selfhood relies upon a group of assumptions about the nature of human life that embody a variety of implicit value judgments. His categories tend to blur distinctions and elude precise definition. His logotherapeutic method has been characterized as a collection of speculations, widely divergent in character and origin and thus exceedingly difficult to identify or validate. The categorical imperative of logotherapy (that one's contemplated actions and decisions should be assumed as potentially wrong and therefore re-examined before deciding) appears to commit man to a specific kind of behavior and may reflect a rather rigid view of human nature. Moreover, the method has been severely attacked for its lack of consistency and failure to provide a sense of workable function—characteristics that are considered vital to behavioral science. If a model is not clear about the ways in which the self functions in its environment, then it is difficult to know what importance or worth the model has for an understanding of human personality.

Frankl's model is made up of three parts: a characterization of human life; a concept of meaning; and the concept of logotherapy. The three parts are so interrelated as to appear somewhat repetitious and in this sense there is considerable lack of precision and distinction in the model.

THE CHARACTERISTICS OF HUMAN LIFE

Frankl finds the contemporary situation of man characterized by a "collective neurosis" that includes an ephemeral and provisional attitude toward everything, a fatalist attitude, a conformist or collectivist mentality and a denial of selfhood. The result of this neurosis is the existential condition of meaninglessness and despair.[1] Frankl called it the existential vacuum within man, a condition that can be supplanted by a set of alternative characteristics.

Three characteristics are said to constitute human life divested of the collective neurosis: man's spirituality, his freedom and his responsibility.[2] For Frankl the self is not determined only by environment and heredity. There is a self-determination or freedom whose primary characteristic is the ability to make decisions about itself. This ability must be cultivated and developed; it does not develop without attention and education but it is the way to stand beyond the bondage to social and hereditary types. The freedom to decide about the self is not a denial or escape from those environmental and hereditary factors that cannot be altered. Rather, freedom is the ability to formulate an attitude toward all the environmental and hereditary factors of human life that cannot be altered.

Frankl's concept of freedom is a basic part of his selfhood model. It is freedom to confront the instincts, inheritance, and the total environment of the organism. It cannot be reduced to more elemental components. A similar condition applies to his concept of responsibility. The self is said to be responsible to its conscience and thus the self-determinative motif is re-emphasized. The responsible self is the self-determinative self.

For Frankl the responsible self is developed in a realization of values. This realization is related to the self's experience of inescapable or unavoidable suffering, of how it is encountered and endured. Suffering is said to be that which is to be borne or endured with fortitude and equanimity. Suffering experienced in this manner is the basis of value realization.

Life has a meaning to the last breath. For the possibility of realizing values by the very attitude with which we face our destined suffering: this possibility is there to the very last moment. I call such values attitudinal values. The right kind of suffering—facing your fate boldly—is the highest achievement which has been granted to man.[3]

Suffering is also the basis of another primary characteristic of the self: the tension between the *is* and the *ought* in human life. The experience of suffering includes a developing awareness of what is and what ought to be and ought not to be in the personality. This provides the basis for additional discrimination or decision about responsibility. To the degree that the self completely identifies with what is, this tension between is and ought is abolished. But for Frankl, the essence of selfhood includes a persistent maintenance of the tension between is and ought. In suffering, in experienced tension between the is and the ought, in freedom and responsibility, the self discovers meaning.

MEANING AND SELFHOOD

Frankl has consistently stressed the primary significance of the will to meaning as an adequate alternative to the existential vacuum he finds so characteristic of contemporary man's life. Meaning is an independent force or

phenomenon characteristic of the self; it is more than self-
actualization or self-expression; it is the result of experiencing values, including the genesis of values in suffering.
Value realization is self-fulfillment or the meaning of
selfhood.

The self's quest for meaning begins with the will to
meaning—an orientation toward meaning as the value
center of human life or selfhood—and proceeds toward a
confrontation with value realization. The continuing experience of confrontation marks the transition from freedom
to responsibleness. Responsible selfhood is a combination
of realized self worth and some additional external goal
or value. The product is meaning or maturity, which appear to be similar terms in Frankl's perspective. Three
interrelated processes characterize meaningful selfhood
and mark its development: (1) what the self gives to
human life; e.g., its creativity, insight, and responsibleness
toward other persons; (2) what the self appropriates from
the world; e.g., values experienced; (3) the stance the self
assumes toward a fate that cannot be altered. Frankl's
methodology for perceiving and initiating this recovery of
meaning and realization of selfhood is a therapeutic endeavor known as logotherapy. Its techniques are based
upon his assumptions about the existential vacuum in
human life and the nature of selfhood as value realization
and the will to meaning.[4]

LOGOTHERAPY

Logotherapy or existential analysis regards man as needing a goal toward which he can work, albeit with striving
and struggling. The quest for a goal, value, or meaning for

the self is the responsibleness that logotherapy affirms as necessary for human life. Its categorical imperative as formulated by Frankl is to "so live as if you were living already for the second time and as if you had acted the first time as wrongly as you are about to act now." [5]

From the phrasing of Frankl's categorical imperative it is possible to conclude that logotherapy is a rather specific, directive and judgmental method. There are obviously some implicit value judgments standing behind the method. It would seem that these judgments (about the nature of man, decision-making, motivation) have remained closed to testing, revision or examination. However, in *The Doctor and the Soul,* he has asserted that logotherapy does not determine or dictate value realization for the self. Rather, logotherapy's task is that of bringing the self to the point of decision about values— to the discernment that decisions are necessary and that some definition of self-responsibility must be made.

Existential analysis, then, does not interfere in the ranking of values; it rests content when the individual begins to evaluate; what values he elects is and remains the patient's own affair. Existential analysis must not be concerned with what the patient decides for, what goals he sets himself, but only that he decides at all.[6]

Another major assertion of logotherapy concerns self-identity or actualization. Frankl claims that self-actualization is possible only to the extent that the will to meaning is fulfilled and values are realized in human life. Self-actualization as an end in itself destroys or seriously impairs the self. Identity and self-actualization function identically in Frankl's language. Man is said to find identity "to the extent to which he commits himself to something beyond himself, to a cause greater than himself." [7] Self-identity centers in a choice or decision about the kind of values and meaning that are affirmed as the goals of human life. These values and goals are not derived from the self as much as from the world and objective reality. Man is thereby said to become what he is according to how he behaves and decides. The world affords him alternative goals and values of which an integrated group ought to be selected and affirmed. In this affirmation selfhood is developed.

Frankl's view of selfhood is to be sharply differentiated from any concept of euphoria, simple harmony, or tensionless existence. It should be recalled at this point that value realization is said to be the product of a decision concerning the tension between what is and what ought to be. The self is characterized by the perpetual reality of this tension between is and ought. Selfhood is not so much discharge of tension as striving for meaning and values that are self-determinative. Selfhood is more self-transcendence than self-actualization. It is the realization of functional values that act to perpetuate human life and to fulfill its quest for meaning. "One characteristic of human existence is its transcendence. That is to say, man transcends his being toward an ought." [8]

FRANKL'S MODEL

Frankl's selfhood model uses a remarkably large number of concepts common to much religious and theological language—conscience, suffering as the basis of responsibility, fate and self-transcendence. Like Fromm, Frankl

started with cultural assumptions emphasizing man's es-
trangement, alienation or aloneness in society—basic
themes for much existential philosophy and theology.
But Frankl's interpretation is considerably closer to those
of the existential theologians than the philosophers or
psychologists.

For example, the basis of self-determination is said
to be a development from the conscience and experiences
of suffering in human life. Another example is Frankl's
goal for selfhood—the will to meaning and self-transcendence. Both of these concepts appear rather consistently
in the history of theology, particularly in many existential
theologians.

Karl Barth, Rudolf Bultmann, Emil Brunner, Reinhold
Niebuhr, Martin Buber, and Gabriel Marcel are all examples of theological emphasis upon meaning and transcendence. A significant exception may be the late Paul
Tillich, whose theology was considerably more neoFreud-
ian and behavioristic than Frankl's psychology. This is
especially the case in terms of self-transcendence and
meaning.

Frankl's explanation of evil says in effect that in retro-
spect man can see that suffering imparted meaning and
purpose to his life. The genesis of man's values is in his
suffering. This argument is a two-part one: (1) a conviction that life has meaning and values; (2) that its
meaning and values can be discovered and attained
through the ways in which man confronts the suffering
and evil that befall him.[9]

The significance of Frankl's analysis for theology and
religion is as an experiential statement or credo. Its basis

Remember that he developed this based on his years in a German concentration camp for Jews

is a reflective interpretation of personal suffering and subsequent comparison with experiences of others. A similar
but perhaps less sanguine analysis has been made by
Langdon Gilkey in his story of internment in a Japanese
concentration camp.[10] Finally, the most publicized theological interpretation of suffering in recent years is that
of Dietrich Bonhoeffer's prison writings.[11] Bonhoeffer's
concept of self-fulfillment attained only at great cost and
endurance emphasizes the hard realities of human existence and the wisdom of not minimizing how difficult a
thing it is to become a whole person. Bonhoeffer was not
as definite as Frankl has been in assigning purposes to
suffering. However, there is an affinity in seeing a connection between suffering and the meaning of selfhood.

Of course, not all theology is in agreement with Frankl's
explanation. For example, another Jewish writer, Rabbi
Richard Rubenstein, who like Frankl begins his analysis
with the experiences of German death camps of World
War II, finds it is utter nonsense to speak of a purpose
in suffering and evil. Attempts to justify or ratify some
sense for suffering and evil are at best serious psychological delusions and at worst twisted and cruel tricks. All
that is humanly necessary or possible is to recognize and
endure whatever suffering befalls us.[12]

Another point at which Frankl's selfhood model bears
some significance for religious thought is in terms of logotherapy. Logotherapy's aim is to bring man to a point
at which he commits himself to some cause beyond himself and his own welfare. Religious aims of conversion are
certainly a similar kind of goal. The principal difference
is that Frankl was not willing to identify a specific con-

tent for self-commitment whereas religious groups are usually quite definite in this respect. Religious thought is likely to find Frankl's position useful in terms of his rationale for "outside" commitment as essential to selfhood. This rationale is the rather vague argument that man is not complete unless committed to some ideal or goal. Man is said to be more noble and of greater worth as he seeks goals beyond his own self-interest. His social origins necessitate a high degree of interdependence with his fellow men and some commitment to their welfare provides an enlarged, more cooperative and responsible pattern of existence. Moreover, such commitments are said to be the precondition of self-identity.

Frankl's value assumptions for selfhood are more explicit and more speculative than those commonly found in behavioral science. They posit a universal fate (a deity?) and a specific set of value choices for human development. Generalizing from personal and clinical experiences, Frankl argues that the will to meaning as a self-transcending goal is validated by suffering and conscience. However, Frankl's methodology as reflected in his writing is a source of considerable confusion. The discourse moves rapidly back and forth and without explicit connectives between clinical observations and reports, philosophical speculations, and attenuated theorizing about the self. It is often difficult to discern when Frankl is reporting, evaluating, or speculating. It is seldom demonstrated how his model and explanation might be tested and validated. The search for meaning is presumably the decisive factor in Frankl's analysis. But we are left with the puzzle of "the meaning of meaning." Is

meaning the all-inclusive category into which all matters
of classifying personality and human development are
collapsed? Confusion of this sort makes it exceedingly
difficult to discern how the self functions in its environment. If these kinds of claims are to be made, then they
are going to have to be argued and not simply asserted
in the way Frankl has done.

The categorical imperative of logotherapy has a judgmental clarity about it. Moreover, it is highly inaccessible
to testing and validation, yet it has been advanced as
a value based upon scientific investigations. We can only
conclude that this kind of imperative does dictate value
realization while itself claiming autonomy and protection
from testing for validation. Again, it is necessary to say
that this kind of claim must be argued and not simply
asserted. Any scientific theory or interpretative model
must give some systematic generalizations that are capable
of empirical testing for validation or modification or
rejection.

It is difficult to determine the meaning of self-transcendence in Frankl's model. It is proposed as an alternative
to self-actualization, but unlike the specified traits of self-
actualizing psychology, self-transcendence is really little
more than a label. Finally, it remains questionable whether
Frankl's values and goals for the self are really derived
from the empirical world and represent significant generalizations. Ultimately they appear to be part of a single
perspective or design that is superimposed upon the self
with little attention paid to the diversity of personality.

5

The INTEGRATED PERSON/Rollo May

New York analyst Rollo May's writings have attracted a wide readership among the general public. One of May's concerns has been to provide useful analysis and self-comprehension for persons in stress. Toward this end he has shown a preference for developing broad social generalizations that are said to be characteristic of a particular time and readily applicable to human life. While these generalizations have varied over several decades, an underlying and consistent theme has been the search for selfhood and identity.

CHARACTERISTICS OF SOCIETY

In writing *Man's Search for Himself* in 1953 May emphasized anxiety, alienation, and loneliness as the dominant characteristics of modern man. Society was said to be experiencing an age of anxiety about everything from wars and death to meeting or not meeting another human being. The result was a destruction of the individual's self-awareness. The roots of this unhappy state of affairs were said to be numerous, including a breakdown in the power of individual reason, an intensified network of interdependence, loss of sense of self-worth, loss of vocabulary for communicating deeply personal meanings, loss of sense of relation to nature and loss of awareness of the tragic element in human existence. This state of accumulated deprivation has resulted in an empty age in which the individual cannot identify himself.

In *Love and Will,* published in 1969, May has reaffirmed the validity of his characterization of the age of emptiness and anxiety. But now it is said that there is

*Is love deliberate, like will?
Could Susan have willed to love
her husband if she had chosen to?*

another critical element involved in the selfhood crisis
and this is a loss of the authentic powers of love and will.
These formerly essential components of stability and identity are now sources of anxiety and isolation. Apathy—
the opposite of love and will—is the characteristic mood
of the present age. It is a time in which the individual
has intense difficulties in finding anything that matters
or is worthy of commitment.

*(Susan) in
Room 19*

In *Love and Will* May also identifies the breakdown
in love to be the result of a "new Puritanism" which consists of a drastic separation of sexuality and sexual relations from eros. This new kind of love consists of an
alienation from the body, a separation of emotion from
reason and use of the body as a machine. Now sexuality
is said to be part of the cult of techniques and efficient
management of human actions. The result is a destruction
of feelings, the undermining of passions and a destruction
of identity.[1] Now modern man is characterized by a loss
of love (eros) and its quality of humaneness which is said
to be essential to selfhood.

SELF-WORTH

A basic sense of self-worth is a characteristic that May
has long identified as essential for selfhood. And thus
value is seen as an essential part of the self. Indeed, May
has gone so far as to suggest that selfhood and identity
are not so much objective traits as a composite of certain
innate convictions and learned values.[2] The fulfillment
and realization of these convictions and values represents
the completed person whose potentials have been fully
achieved.

*if they are honest convictions
+ values, not just c. + v. imposed
by tradition, habits, parents, etc.*

Foremost among these potentials is self-worth, which is a composite characteristic. It involves: (1) achievement of self-consciousness and discovery of feelings; (2) a rediscovery of the body and integration of self and the body; (3) movement toward what one wants from human life; (4) a rediscovery of the subconscious dimensions of the self. The cumulative result of these factors equals one's self-worth. May's high valuation of self-worth points to a more general value judgment for his perspective of the self and society: That "the more self-awareness a person has, the more alive he is." [3] Fundamental to this assertion and to all of May's writings about selfhood is the concept of integration and wholeness. Self-worth is a composite trait whose key is an integration or wholeness of the components. Similarly, his selfhood goals are related to each other in terms of the concept of integration and wholeness.

GOALS OF THE INTEGRATED SELF

Human life is regarded by May as a continuing struggle to differentiate and integrate a variety of goals. Foremost among these are four interrelated ones: (1) freedom and inner strength; (2) creative conscience; (3) courage; (4) transcendence of time.

Freedom is said to be the self's degree of capacity to manage its own development. It is a cumulative experience achieved daily in the extent to which the individual affirms and assumes responsibility for selfhood. This characteristic is formed in how the self relates to the determined and fixed aspects of reality. The continuing result is a strengthening of the self's resolve to affirm freedom or a pattern of progressive resignation, loss of self-determination, and an erratic pattern of relating to the fixed, intractable parts of reality.

Creative conscience reflects May's conviction that persons have a fundamental potential for ethical judgment and action. He has spoken of a "core of integration," a psychic core, and a "psychological center" of the self.[4] This is the consciousness of the self and it is said to bear the template or picture and impression of values that can be put into practice by the person. Of course the degree of realization of this potential is directly related to the relative inner strength and freedom of the self in the face of social pressures for conformity, control, and obedience without reason. On the one hand, the creative conscience requires the selfhood goals of freedom and inner strength for its achievement while on the other hand, the conscience provides form, substance, and action to freedom.

Courage is the capacity to deal with the anxiety generated in the struggle for freedom and self-determination. It is an inner condition or trait that develops out of self-confidence and is closely related to the sense of self-worth. It is a capacity to recognize and affirm truth about the self. May cites Paul Tillich's ideal of the ability to trust the self made in the complete awareness of the self's limitations as an example of courage. It is a fundamental characteristic of self-development in an age when social control and personal isolation are such dominant forces.

The fourth and final goal of May's integrated self is its ability to transcend time. This involves the ability to live in the reality of the present without excessive escape into the past or anticipation of the future. Underlying this goal is May's implicit conviction that the self is dependent upon a variety of things of which time is of relatively minor importance. *Man's Search for Himself* contains an extended discussion of eternity as a way of relating to human life. In terms paralleling those of Spinoza and Tillich, May speaks of self-integration as an act within the form of eternity.[5] This metaphysical vision concludes the discussion of the goals of selfhood and reaffirms the fundamental nature of value for the self. Unfortunately it does so without explicating or arguing the case.

In *Love and Will* May has added the recovery of love and will as goals for the integrated self. Again the emphasis is upon integrating these items. That is to say, both love and will are ways of relating to reality and they must be joined together at all times if there is to be balance and health. The uniting of love and will is spoken of as the fundamental task of the self. In respect to both traits, May introduces a number of value issues and judgments. Love is said to be a unique characteristic of human life that must be recovered by modern man. It is the humane quality that has significant value in existence. Similarly, will is said to be fundamental to the self. The paralysis of will in modern man is a result of his technical and mechanical creations as well as anxiety and isolation. A recovery of will is necessary to enrich human existence as well as to provide an adequate and controlled basis of power. Dignity, respect for life, depth and meaning of existence, and similar value terms punctuate May's discussion of love and will and are asserted to be the preferred characteristics of selfhood.

MAY'S MODEL

Rollo May has explicitly spoken of the parallel relationships and similarities between existential philosophies and
his psychoanalytic perspective of the self. Particularly significant are the common concerns to overcome the subject-
object dichotomy in describing man, the developmental
or emergent concept of human nature, and the conviction
that crisis (not despair) is a constant factor in existence.[6]
Moreover, May's perspective has shown a consistent preference for value concepts as fundamental characteristics
of the self (e.g., depth of human existence, dignity, respect
for human life, and courage). In this respect it is similar
to the models developed by a variety of existential philosophers and theologians. Another area of similarity is the
tendency to describe selfhood in terms of metaphysical
and theological concepts such as a universal structure of
reality, eternity, transcendence, the Logos, and the power
of the demonic.

May has made love a matter of foremost concern and
in this respect his model holds particular interest for religious thought. May's interpretation is a straightforward
one, although it remains to be seen if it is valid: That
love as eros is significantly lacking in this age and must
be recovered if man is to know himself and gain his well-
being. He asserts that love has been replaced by apathy
that leads to the absence of self-commitment and a loss
of ability to survive.

In Western culture, discussions of love have tended to
distinguish between two kinds of love—agape and eros.
Agape generally denotes the love of a god for mankind,

brotherly love among people, or some kind of spiritual love. It is love without sexual, bodily, and sensual implications, meanings, or intentions. In contrast, eros speaks of a variety of kinds of human love, including bodily, sexual love among persons. In recent usage eros has often come to mean love that seeks human fulfillment (including sexual fulfillment) without causing injury to others. This last usage is May's general meaning of eros-type love.

Love has often been the subject of theological reflection and in recent years this interest has been intensified. Anders Nygren developed a large-scale systematic theological examination of love in *Agape and Eros*.[7] After exploring the differences between the two kinds of love, Nygren devoted his attention to developing the meaning and implications of agape. Agape is presented as the model toward which human life should aspire. It is a self-giving, brotherly, servant-like, spiritual model for human relationships. Paul Tillich has explored the relationships of agape to power and justice in society and has illuminated the intricate interrelationships between the three.[8] Reuel Howe has explored the relationships of agape and eros to the workings of churches and the interpersonal relationships of individuals and communities.[9] Joseph Fletcher has sought to establish love as the foundation of ethics and morality with his "situation ethics." Love is defined as a predicate rather than a property or thing and it is mankind's fundamental guide to the good.[10] Jules Toner has surveyed the meanings of love in theological history, James Gustafson has analyzed the theological relationships of freedom and love, and Daniel Day Williams has written an extensive systematic work that depicts and explores the major theological topics related to love.[11]

While most of these theologians have been careful to distinguish between agape and eros, and have taken agape to be their primary concern, there are some ties between them and Rollo May's concern for the recovery of love. Specifically, May and Paul Tillich share a common concern for an intelligent and humane use of love, power, and justice that stresses the mutual relationships of the three. May and Howe share a concern for the ultimate importance of love in all aspects of interpersonal relationships. And May and Fletcher share a common affirmation of love's necessity in fostering the good. Although Fletcher speaks of love in terms of agape and consistently ties his use to Christian matters, there would appear to be a rather broad similarity between his definition of Christian love as "benevolence" and "goodwill" and May's concept of love as the balancing force in society.[12] Underlying all these matters is a common conviction concerning love's fundamental importance for selfhood. A multitude of meanings for emotions, feelings, concerns, and cares intersect with one another under the label of love. And while the diversity of definitions often seems to be as significant if not more so than the similarities, there seems to be little question about the essential impact and force of love in the development of selfhood.

In summarizing, if we are to evaluate the significance of Rollo May's contribution to an understanding of the self, we need to mention a number of things. Certainly the emphasis upon love is a significant "reading" of man's development and his struggle to identify himself. In this emphasis May's work is similar to that of much religious thought in the Judeo-Christian tradition as well as many psychological views. His difference and identifying characteristic is the emphasis upon eros and the need for its recovery in the present age. The emphasis May places upon an integrated or whole person is common to much psychology and religion. More problematical for psychology, is May's reliance upon certain values and theological ideas that are never entirely clear. For example, courage, dignity, depth, and meaning are said to be important parts of the self but we are never really given a psychological explanation of these matters. How do they function? What is their origin? How do they differ from each other? Of equal uncertainty is how the conscience acquires its basic set of values in May's model. Values are said to be innately inherent in persons but this does not explain their origin and nature or why there is such an immense diversity of values among people.[13] The end result is a model that emphasizes some significant issues of the personality—in particular the identity quest of contemporary psychological man—but does not give a full (integrated?) and clearly reasoned view of selfhood.

A final item concerns May's age of new Puritanism in which sexual techniques are sought at the expense of love. This suggests a critical dichotomy between feelings and technology. And it suggests the dangers of a new religious technology in which tools and techniques are valued and practiced at the expense of religious experience.

6

The SELF-ACTUALIZING PERSON/Abraham Maslow

Abraham Maslow directed his psychological investigations toward the healthy personality and the quest for selfhood. In doing this he reported on the incidence of a set of traits that constitute a model for the healthy or normal self. This is the so-called self-actualizing personality that has been the subject of so much controversy since its introduction to the behavioral science vocabulary. Maslow's work is significant because it asserted that certain values and meanings about the self are part of the empirical data of this research. In particular, Maslow was convinced that the normal or healthy personality is the self-actualizing personality.

In *Motivation and Personality* he suggested that we now have a species-wide definition of normal and healthy based upon three propositions deduced from the study of persons: (1) that man has an essential nature or self of his own (such as the self-actualizing personality to be described); (2) that health and normalcy consist in actualizing man's essential nature or self; (3) that psychological illness results from denial, frustration, or twisting of man's nature. These propositions and their supporting data provide explicit redefinitions of the good, the normal, and the healthy personality.

What is good? Anything that conduces to this desirable development in the direction of actualization of the inner nature of man. What is bad or abnormal? Anything that frustrates or blocks or denies the essential nature of man. What is psychopathological? Anything that disturbs or frustrates or twists the course of self-actualization.[1]

THE TRAITS OF SELF-ACTUALIZATION

Maslow's model for selfhood was a collection or set of traits found to exist with more or less consistency in a range of people studied over a period of years. The traits of the self-actualizing person include efficient perception of reality and comfortable relations with it, acceptance of self, others and nature without threat, spontaneity in behavior, a strong focusing on problems outside the self (problem centered rather than ego centered), a quality of detachment and need for privacy, relative autonomy of physical and social environment, a continued freshness of appreciation of self, others and nature, a sense of a mystic (William James) or oceanic (Sigmund Freud) experience as a natural and not a theological phenomenon, a sense of identity, feeling and friendliness for others and the world, meaningful interpersonal relationships, a democratic character structure, consistent ability to regard ends as more important than means, an unhostile sense of humor toward the world, creativeness, resistance to enculturation, and a certain inner detachment from culture.

These traits are not so much a path or guide to self-actualization as they are an inventory of the basic qualities found by Maslow's empirical studies. What these traits do indicate is the distinctive motivational life of self-actualizing people.

The motivational life of self-actualizing people is not only quantitatively but also qualitatively different from that of ordinary people. It seems probable that we must construct a profoundly different psychology of motivation for self-actualizing people; e.g., expression motivation or growth motivation rather than deficiency motivation.[2]

The self-actualizing personality displays a distinctive holism by which the usual dichotomies of personality are merged into a larger pattern. Personality dichotomies are bridged but in no way should this be confused with a simplistic balancing, equilibrium of well-being, or state of suspended activity. Such a state, as applied to personality, is a circular concept by which human life is reduced to a series of tension reductions, eventuating in a semipassive, changeless state. In contrast, the self-actualizing personality is a dynamic whole that bridges the usual dichotomies of personality, holding them in tension with one another. The id, ego, and superego are said to be collaborative rather than divisive in these people. Dichotomies are either resolved or held in a tolerable tension in the self-actualizing personality. What this is said to demonstrate is the inadequacy of dichotomizing as a way of depicting the healthy self.

In his later work Maslow redefined self-actualization as a biologically based inner nature, partly unique to the individual and partly species wide. This inner nature is not intrinsically evil but neutral or good, and evil represents a frustration of this good. The goal of selfhood is development of this inner nature.[3] The primary empirical expressions of the self's inner nature are so-called peak experiences. A number of values and traits characterize a peak experience including truth, goodness, beauty, wholeness, aliveness, uniqueness, perfection, completion,

justice, simplicity, richness, effortlessness, playfulness and
self-sufficiency.[4] Maslow's redefinition of self-actualization
actually allows for a limited incidence of the phenomenon
in a wide range of personalities that are not consistently
self-actualizing. The peak experience is like an episode or
incident in human life in which self-actualization occurs,
usually for a limited duration. This modification recog-
nizes a diversity within personality and makes self-actualization a more flexible model than many of Maslow's
critics thought and claimed.

SELF-ACTUALIZATION AND VALUE

Maslow's investigations were concerned with value, a matter that he consistently claimed as an integral part of
psychology's scientific investigation. Self-actualization is
a value—a kind of goal toward which personality strives
and the significance of which is the full realization of selfhood in human life. For Maslow there was a descriptive,
naturalistic science of human values whose content is the
self-actualizing process.

The paradox of Maslow's model and its system of
values arises with respect to the goal of self-actualization.
The goal is an end in itself and also a transition or rite
of passage in self-development. Self-actualization's function is almost like saying that it strives to erase itself,
in order for the full personality to develop and enlarge its
health and well-being. Self-actualization as *the* value of
selfhood is not a tensionless, euphoric state but a "development of personality which frees the person from the
neurotic problems of life so that he is able to face, endure,
and grapple with the real problems of life." [5]

In regard to individual values and ethics, Maslow reported that self-actualizing persons have a distinctive pattern of behavior and conduct. It is largely autonomous and individual rather than conventional. Their ethics are based upon principles that are perceived to be true and basic to human existence. These principles are applied to situations and decisions are then made regarding actions. The consistent factors in the ethical decision-making of self-actualizing persons are a striving to translate into immediate actions what has been perceived as true and an ability to withstand pressures for conformity and adherence to conventional patterns of behavior. They seldom show in their "day-to-day living the chaos, the confusion, the inconsistency, or the conflict that are so common in the average person's ethical dealings." [6] Finally, they are most often concerned with ends rather than means, although this is a matter requiring careful qualification. In particular, the self-actualizing person tends to see the means-end identification as a complex matter in most situations. In general, they often see as ends specific experiences and actions that other people would regard as means. Thus they could be said to have a highly developed sense of responsibility and concern for the application of truth to all experiences and actions.

MASLOW'S MODEL

Like Gordon Allport, Abraham Maslow was intent upon adhering to strict canons of behavioral science in exploring the nature of selfhood. And thus his generalizations are the expression of data subject to verification and testing. Similarly, his model places a premium upon clarity and precision of concepts. The result is a well-defined model that attempts accurately to summarize his empirical findings. In this respect the model is to be differentiated from those that rely heavily upon valuational and metaphysical concepts.

Fundamentally, Maslow defined value as whatever promotes or creates the self-actualizing personality. This suggests a naturalistic science of human values. However, it is important to see that Maslow's model included an implicit value judgment whereby a basic kind of personality (the self-actualizing one) was regarded as superior to all others. Maslow's defense of this judgment was that the empirical data substantiated this personality as the one that was most capable of sustained endurance, effective adjustment to reality, and maintenance of harmonious existence. Essentially Maslow regarded a species wide definition of selfhood to be substantiated by his data.

This concept of selfhood is at variance with much theology in terms of its concept of man's nature and goals. For Maslow, this nature was really neutral and neither good or evil. The history of theology does not show this clear and distinct a consensus of opinion. Sometimes rather hastily and by verbal assertions theologians have seen man as a sinner, as not basically inclined toward the good, or as inclined toward evil.[7] Of course there are theological distinctions ad infinitum between evil, sin, and sinning and I am not suggesting that they represent identical images of man. But we do need to recognize that *in general* ideas of man as a sinner, as "fallen," as less than his worth, or as evil and debased stand in contrast to Maslow's perception of man as neutral.

More to the point, however, is that much Christian theology has shown a divided mind about man. That is to say, on the one hand, theologians have often seen the "imago dei," the "little Christ" in everyman (Luther), and on the other hand, have seen man as hopelessly lost in sin and forever unable to "do the good that I will" (Paul). Such a both/and viewpoint is not the same thing as Maslow's neutrality, for it usually includes the assertion that man has the potential for good, but in and of himself is incapable of achieving it. This is close to the position taken by Augustine in his *Confessions,* which is probably one of the more sophisticated pieces of religious psychology ever written. Similar positions have been taken by a variety of recent theologians including Karl Barth, Emil Brunner, Reinhold Niebuhr, and Rudolf Bultmann. The self, theologically speaking, has often been depicted as needing some outside help to move toward the good and become complete. Man has been seen as somewhat tragic in that he so often fails to realize the good and is in constant need of major assistance to avoid evil. In contrast, Maslow's model displays a steadfast confidence in man's self-sufficiency and self-actualization. The questions of divine assistance and powers beyond the human ability are not part of Maslow's concept of the self.

Another example of Maslow's emphasis upon human self-sufficiency can be seen in his handling of love. As we have already noted in discussing Rollo May's idea of love, theologians have tended to emphasize agape as a model and ideal for human love. Maslow was not interested in the distinctions between agape and eros; rather, he was intent upon describing love's nature in the self-actualizing personality. Among the characteristics of this love are an absence of defensiveness, a sense of being loved and of giving love, a pooling of the needs of two persons into a single pattern of needs, an ability to accept and respect the individuality of the partner, a perception and affirmation of love as an end experience (never a means), and a full merging of sexuality and love.

Maslow's description of love emphasized the quality of openness to others and increasing spontaneity toward them.[8] The total quality of love is said to be essential to the self-actualizing person. Thus there is a concern to see that love does not manipulate or control others. It is a merging of love and respect that characterizes the self-actualizing person's relationships with others. Similarly, love and affection are said to be necessary for experiences of sexuality in self-actualizing people.

While much of Maslow's description of love does not sound that different from those of the theologians, it is fundamentally different in its origin and interpretation of the values of love. Maslow saw no divine origin, ideal, or analogy between self-actualizing love and another form, such as agape. The values of love are fully human and social values and not analogies of a divine pattern. Love's basis and importance lies in itself as an experience and not as a derivative of another experience or power.

Maslow's work must be commended for its attempt to seek a theory of values related to the nature of personality. Here we can note an earnest attempt to discover not only what man is but what he can become. Moreover, in this model there is the insight that the self can be much healthier than its culture. And while most persons are probably not totally self-actualizing at all times, the attainment of values not bound to the culture is shown to be possible. In any age this capability is an exceedingly important one—a kind of psychological distance by which the self can develop and maintain a coherent life pattern (such as self-actualization) irrespective of the pressures and forces exerted by the culture. Equally significant is the place that Maslow's research is increasingly being accorded in behavioral science. His "third force" is regarded as a systematic alternative to two dominating systems of contemporary psychology—those of Sigmund Freud and C. J. Jung.[9] Maslow's third force places its fundamental emphasis on the positive side of man's needs, goals, and achievements.

Another of the positive attributes of Maslow's model— its availability for testing—is also one of its critical problems. That is, perhaps there has not yet been sufficient testing of the model in large, diverse samples of people. The greater percentage of Maslow's sample was made up of people drawn from two or three kinds of environments rather than from a large cross section of society. A more serious and elusive dilemma is that of the initial selection of people for testing. This raises in a new way the problem of defining healthy or normal. Did Maslow adopt the absence of treatment as his method of evaluation? How can we be content with samples made up of those "who seem to be normal?" The underlying question here is

whether there are presuppositions about health and normalcy that may have prematurely defined what Maslow's
data was said to define.

Maslow also emphasized the importance of making a
distinction between scientific empiricism and technology.
The consequences of psychological or religious technology
are an expertise in the application of tools and techniques,
often at the expense of other ways of understanding and
solving problems. In comparison, empiricism is more an
outlook, a methodology or way of comprehending the
world and attempting to find out what exists. Its first question is "what is" whereas technology usually begins by
asking what can be made, changed, or restructured.

There are manifold dangers in a fascination with technology and tools in either psychology or religion. The sub-
stitution of tools and techniques for experiences and scientific knowledge leads to a life in which the prior issues
of what is and how we determine what will be are never
really examined. If the understanding of selfhood is con-
verted to a technological enterprise, then the whole complex life of the organism is likely to be ignored and
questions of species-wide definition and validity are side-
stepped.

A significant characteristic of Maslow's model—like
Gordon Allport's—is the emphasis placed on empirical
study, testing and validation of generalizations and observations. Generalizations without substantiating evidence
are hardly credible. Maslow and Allport demanded empirical anchors to confirm or deny any generalization.
Value judgments were examined and tested in terms of

their origins, functions, and content with an eye to their consistency, coherence, and basis in evidence. Caution was taken to avoid carelessly converting individual subjective judgments into generalizations and models. The goal of such a method is a more comprehensive species-wide understanding of selfhood based upon substantiating evidence and capable of validation in repeated study and testing.

Maslow's model presents an optimistic picture of the self and its potentialities for growth and development. As with all models, one should not be disparaging of this trait. It is more useful to be respectfully skeptical, asking only that the model be subjected to continued testing in order that the quest for a more accurate and adequate view of selfhood is the result of all investigation.

7

SELFHOOD in PSYCHOLOGY and RELIGION

At the beginning I said that all who seek to explore the relationships of psychology and religion must do so with considerable caution and hesitation. I hope these comments on modern ideas of the self have clarified and substantiated that warning. There have been many books written by theologians and pastoral psychologists about this relationship. Some have been popular and some have not, but in my estimation most of them have been too simplistic, too eager to seek the similarities, and far too timid in making clear the fundamental differences and oppositions between the two fields.[1] The relationships between psychology and religion are complex and intricate matters, and within that domain probably one of the most amorphous and elusive matters is that of the self. And yet it is with the self that modern religion and psychology have been most intensively and intimately concerned. Perhaps even the common concerns of this quest have contributed to the intensity of the pursuit and its often heated disagreements. What I hope to do here is to summarize the major points at issue that have emerged and then mention several areas of exploration that might open up new discussion.

SOME COMMON CHARACTERISTICS

In general, some common characteristics can be seen in the six psychological models for selfhood. There is a common concern for defining the elements of human development and exploring exactly how they fit together as a selfhood model. Similarly, there is interest in the nature of society and its interactions with the self. As a consequence of this concern, all six models seek to define the meaning and implications of individual and social freedom in the modern world. Underlying all of these characteristics is the common element of a quest to define health in the self and society. And as a consequence, there is common concern for the functional operation of society on an ordered, smoothly run basis. Inasmuch as it is possible to generalize, these characteristics provide a basic core or profile of modern psychological models of selfhood.

As I have pointed out at various points, it is only in rather vague and general ways that these characteristics can be said to be parallel or similar to those of religious and theological images of the self. Naturally the degree of similarity or divergence varies immensely with the article of religious thought or practice selected for comparison. Certainly concepts of freedom and concern for individual and social well-being are to be found throughout religious history and thought. But the degree of commonalty and general agreement about characteristics is immeasurably less cohesive or prevalent than in the behavioral sciences.

In contrast to theological ideas of man and selfhood, the new psychological models are largely devoid of metaphysical issues and methods, and this must certainly be counted as one of their important distinguishing characteristics. Moreover, there appears to be little direct exploration of the meaning and implications of man's relationship to nature and the earth. To be certain, this relationship is presupposed, but its significance really has not been explored. Similarly, the implications of mystery and fantasy in human life are largely ignored in the six models. In contrast, perhaps the place of greatest parallel between these models and those of philosophy or religion is in terms of their affinity with the existential images of man.*

By now it should be clear that it is simply not possible to make any easy or extensive claims for the similarity between psychology and religion in the matter of understanding human nature. To be certain, there are similarities and parallels but there are equally, if not more important differences, and these cannot be glossed over. In some very important respects—particularly in terms of basic or core characteristics—I would suggest that religion has much to learn from the models of the behavioral sciences. And conversely, in other vital respects—particularly in terms of mystery, fantasy and the human relationships to nature—the behavioral sciences could profit from the perspectives of literature and religion. There is no easy reduction of the issues to a few common elements. Nevertheless, the explorations of selfhood can profit from an openness in methods and a willingness to consider all the diverse data of human experience.

THE METHODOLOGICAL ISSUES

In terms of methods the models show considerable diversity, the most fundamental difference being that between the strictly empirical, the semi-empirical, and the specula-

---

* To make this comparison see, for example, Nathan A. Scott, *The Unquiet Vision: Mirrors of Man in Existentialism,* New York, World Publishing Company, 1970.

tive, existential types. Allport's and Maslow's models are perhaps the most strictly empirical of the group in comparison with the more speculative, semi-popular ones of Fromm, Frankl, and May. Somewhere in between these is Erikson's clinically based theoretical model. At the root of this diversity is a set of judgments concerning the nature of behavioral science. Intimately related to these complex judgments are fundamental presuppositions concerning human abilities and range of cognitive skill. The result is the vital differences seen in these models.

However, beyond the diversity of methods there are some important common methodological elements in the models. One of these is the tendency not to differentiate too sharply between nature and history. In general, to the behavioral scientist the self is a more or less unified organism that must be studied in the light of this empirical reality. And this includes a recognition that nature and history are combined in the self's experiences and any attempt to sharply differentiate between them is artificial and more fictional than realistic. Here is one of the most elemental and significant differences between theological and psychological models of the self. Theologies of many varieties throughout history have tended to make rather severe distinctions between nature and history under a variety of methods and systems. And it is in this respect that the theologian's great difficulties in recognizing and incorporating dynamic, psychological dimensions into his model can be seen. The result often has been highly speculative, nonempirical, one-dimensional, artificial models of the self.

Related to the nature-history problem is another characteristic in which the six models show a fundamental basis of accord. This is a strenuous effort to dispel and counter the force of repression in understanding the self. To many behavioral scientists, attempts to completely master the inner or outer world are unhealthy and often damaging repressions. Certainly massive repressive energy is required to control or manage reality, to "fit" the self and reality into a simple, easily grasped pattern, or to divide reality into a variety of more manageable components. The result of such efforts is inevitably a form of regression born of a compulsion to see everything completed, finalized, and closed. Such efforts are never very effective, for reality seldom conforms to any one pattern and the behavior of others cannot be entirely controlled. Thus the self that attempts to complete or finalize everything can only do so by ignoring or repressing everything that does not fit into the pattern. And in this way the self gets further and further out of contact with things as they are in the world.

To many behavioral scientists, religious doctrines seem to be a kind of repression. For example, a dictation theory of biblical interpretation that includes such beliefs as creation of the world in six, twenty-four-hour days denies the facts of empirical science. Holding such beliefs involves repression that can seriously impair the self's ability to live in the present age. This is an elementary example, but the principle is one that is involved in all kinds of issues in which psychologists look at religious beliefs and practices.[2] The matter is a point of significant difference between theological and scientific models for selfhood. In terms of methodological starting points, it is one of the most extensive and wide-ranging problems. Like all the methodological issues, it plays a major role in determining the image and goals of man.

THE IMAGE OF MAN

At least three different images of man and his destiny can be seen in the six models: There is the perspective that sees no higher power than the self in the world (Fromm). Then there is the perspective that sees man possessing some power of transcendence (Frankl and May). Finally, there is the perspective that sees man as essentially a neutral and natural organism, a product of the earth and child of his environment (Erikson, Allport, Maslow). The differences these perspectives represent in terms of the goals and values for selfhood provide a useful summary of the characteristics of models. They provide some indicators of what seems possible for the self and society and they give us an insight into man's real and imagined enemies.

For some models, man's foremost enemy is religion as a kind of universal neurosis and the transference kind of God it projects. In a uniquely original book on psychology and religion, *Theology After Freud,* Peter Homans has argued that one of the real differences between psychology and religion lies in their response to man's enemies and their methods of reparation.[3] It is this view of man, his enemies, his goals, and destiny that quickly distinguishes and summarizes the essence of the selfhood models.

TRANSCENDENCE AND PSYCHOLOGICAL MAN

A fundamental issue in any image of man is the relative power and destiny of the self, a matter in which the six models show real diversity. The issue of transcendence—of man's potential power to extend beyond himself, to outdistance or outlive his humanness—is the point of critical parting of the ways. And in one way or another transcendence has long been a basic characteristic of theological models. For many behavioral scientists transcendence represents an authoritarian and compulsive exercise of will, a myth of fiction, and an artificial conception that bears no relation to reality and cannot be validated. On these terms, the religious or psychological model that adopts transcendence—in whatever form—plays a role in society of cultivating and sustaining a cultural superego, a kind of myth that has inadequate backing and justification for its existence.

If we press this disagreement, two immediate alternatives come into view. On the one hand, it is possible to regard religion's job as that of analyzing and interpreting religious images such as transcendence. Now, if from the viewpoint of a scientific culture these images no longer exist, then at least for some people the value of religion will be exceedingly dubious. On the other hand, it is possible to see religion's job as providing aid and support for a kind of moral psychology of modern society. This becomes the practice of the possible in the light of the collapse of the old religious images (like transcendence) under the press of demands for verification. Obviously neither of these alternatives is especially congenial to pro-

ponents of religion and theology, although both have been
suggested and developed in the behavioral sciences.

Of course there may be more alternatives to modern
man's transcendence dilemma. Peter Homans has argued
for a kind of psychological hermeneutic in which images
are seen as at once theological and psychological. Using
the concept of distance, he posits a connection between
theological concepts like transcendence and psychological
concepts like insight, recollection, and comprehension.
In this connection there is an attempt to see the collapse
of transcendence as opening up a shift in comprehension
of the self from an idea of self-limitation to one of self-
completion.⁴ What then emerges is a plurality of master
images that are never reduced or closed into a single
master image. In a manner reminiscent of the metaphysical idea of "prehensions" created by the late philosopher
Alfred North Whitehead, Homans argues that the solution
of these matters lies in a psychoanalytic "impulse to com-
plicate, to expand, to enrich, to double back and look
again and again—not to deny closure or commitment, but
to make possible the suspension of closure in the interests
of something more." ⁵ And much of that "something
more" is an intent and ability to know exactly how we are
related to the past so as to know where we are going and
not to repeat our errors and tragedies. This suggests that
man's destiny is self-completion rather than a transcendence that closes and finalizes everything. It is another
model for selfhood in this age of psychological man.

Another alternative is Robert Lifton's model of protean
man, which is a rather epoch breaking model that goes

far toward analyzing and comprehending man in this age. Briefly stated, protean man is understood as an emerging psychological life style of extensive proportions in both Eastern and Western cultures. Protean man's life is characterized by easy shifts in beliefs and identifications rooted in endless searching, exploration, and flux in all areas of human experience. He can rather easily identify with a variety of beliefs, ideas, and symbols but he has immense difficulty sustaining any prolonged allegiance or connection with these. Protean man has a deep inner sense of absurdity that expresses itself in a "prevailing tone of mockery. His mockery in fact is a specific rejection of moral earnestness and rectitude, a means of giving voice to the absence of 'fit' between inner and outer words so characteristic of our era." [6] As if in response to himself, protean man is also an incurable seeker after a kind of symbolic immortality and rebirth. It is his attempt to synthesize and manage the tensions of a self that exists between life and death.

Lifton's model is perhaps the most comprehensive one developed in response to the quest for selfhood in this age of psychological man. It provides some extensive and insightful clues to the nature of this age and offers a persuasive alternative to the issues of transcendence, identity, and selfhood. In any future considerations about selfhood, it will have to be mentioned and taken very intently.

To conclude, however the issues of transcendence and selfhood are depicted, it remains apparent that there are critical differences alongside the similarities between psychological and religious models for selfhood. To prematurely close the debate on these matters is to arbitrarily settle them with little regard to the evidence or complexities of the case at hand. The search for selfhood demands a continuing exploration of the evidence and a willingness to explore the manifold differences and similarities without diluting or minimizing their relative significance. Finally, it demands a recognition that whatever one's ultimate loyalties, the self is a complex living organism whose nature, form, and substance can only be partially represented in any model.

NOTES

1. ADULTHOOD AND IDENTITY

1. Erik Erikson, 1950: *Childhood and Society,* New York City, W. W. Norton and Company, p. 239.
2. Erik Erikson, 1959: *Identity and the Life Cycle,* New York City, International Universities Press, pp. 55–56.
3. Erikson, *Childhood and Society,* p. 223.
4. Erikson, *Identity and the Life Cycle,* p. 68.
5. *Ibid.,* p. 81.
6. *Ibid.,* p. 85.
7. *Ibid.,* p. 89.
8. *Ibid.,* p. 95.
9. *Ibid.,* p. 96.
10. *Ibid.*
11. *Ibid.,* p. 97.
12. *Ibid.,* p. 98.
13. For example, Paul Tillich, Reinhold Niebuhr, Erich Frank, and Richard Rubenstein. Paul Tillich, 1952, *The Courage to Be,* Yale University Press; Reinhold Niebuhr, 1941, *The Nature and Destiny of Man;* 1955, *The Self and the Dramas of History, Scribners;* Erich Frank, 1945, *Philosophical Understanding and Religious Truth,* Oxford University Press; Richard Rubenstein, 1966, *After Auschwitz,* and 1968, *The Religious Imagination,* Bobbs-Merrill.
14. Paul Tillich, 1952, *The Courage to Be,* p. 181.
15. *Ibid.*
16. Erik Erikson, 1958: *Young Man Luther,* New York City, W. W. Norton Company, p. 210.
17. *Ibid.,* p. 214.
18. *Ibid.,* p. 217.
19. *Ibid.,* p. 261.
20. *Ibid.,* p. 262.
21. *Ibid.,* p. 264.

22. Paul Tillich, *The Courage to Be,* p. 189.
23. Erik Erikson, 1968: *Identity: Youth and Crisis,* New York City, W. W. Norton and Company, p. 293.

2. THE AUTONOMOUS SELF

1. Gordon Allport, 1955: *Becoming,* New Haven, Yale University Press, pp. 9–12.
2. Gordon Allport, 1961: *The Individual and His Religion,* New York City, Macmillan, pp. 23–25.
3. Gordon Allport, 1968: *The Person in Psychology,* Boston, Beacon Press, pp. 149–50.
4. Allport, *The Individual and His Religion,* p. 57.
5. *Ibid.,* p. 116.
6. Gordon Allport, 1961: *Pattern and Growth in Personality,* New York City, Holt, Reinhart and Winston, p. 250.
7. Gordon Allport, 1960: *Personality and Social Encounter,* Boston, Beacon Press, p. 35.
8. *Ibid.,* p. 161.
9. See Allport's *Pattern and Growth in Personality* for a complete discussion of the proprium.
10. Allport, *Becoming,* pp. 27–28.
11. Allport, *The Individual and His Religion,* p. 142.
12. Allport, *The Person in Psychology,* p. 406.

3. THE SOCIAL ROOTS OF SELFHOOD

1. Erich Fromm, 1941: *Escape From Freedom,* New York City, Holt, Reinhart and Winston, pp. 16–17.
2. Erich Fromm, 1964: *The Heart of Man,* New York City, Harper & Row, p. 23.
3. *Ibid.,* pp. 105–8.
4. Fromm, *Escape From Freedom,* p. 36.
5. *Ibid.,* pp. 138–39.
6. Erich Fromm, 1950: *Psychoanalysis and Religion,* New Haven, Yale University Press, pp. 74–79.

7. Fromm, *Escape From Freedom,* pp. 104–19.
8. Erich Fromm, 1955: *The Dogma of Christ and Other Essays on Religion, Psychology, and Culture,* New York City, Holt, Reinhart and Winston, p. 157.
9. Fromm, *Escape From Freedom,* p. 265.
10. Helmut Kuhn, 1949: *Encounter With Nothingness,* Chicago, Henry Regnery Company, p. 39.
11. See *Man's Nature and His Communities,* 1965, New York City, Scribners, especially pp. 106–8.
12. H. Richard Niebuhr, 1963: *The Responsible Self,* New York City, Harper & Row.
13. James M. Gustafson, 1961: *Treasure in Earthen Vessels,* New York City, Harper & Row and 1970, *The Church as Moral Decision-maker,* Philadelphia, Pilgrim Press.
14. Waldo Beach, 1969: *Christian Community and American Society,* Philadelphia, The Westminster Press, especially chapters 3, 6, 7, 8, 9.
15. Julian N. Hartt, 1967: *A Christian Critique of American Culture,* New York City, Harper & Row and Rubem Alves, 1969, *A Theology of Human Hope,* New York City, Corpus Books. For a more complete analysis of these issues also see, Theodore A. McConnell, 1970, "Theological Agendas for the Seventies," *Religious Education,* Vol. 65, No. 6.
16. See especially his *The Phenomenon of Man, The Future of Man, Hymn of the Universe,* and *Man's Place in Nature,* Harper & Row.

4. THE QUEST FOR MEANING

1. Viktor Frankl, 1967: *Psychotherapy and Existentialism,* New York City, Washington Square Press, pp. 84 ff.
2. Viktor Frankl, 1965: *The Doctor and the Soul,* New York City, Alfred A. Knopf, p. xviii; and 1955: "The Concept of Man in Psychotherapy" in *Pastoral Psychology,* 6(58), p. 22.
3. Frankl, "The Concept of Man in Psychotherapy," p. 18.
4. Frankl, *Psychotherapy and Existentialism,* p. 11.

5. Viktor Frankl, 1959: *Man's Search for Meaning,* Boston, Beacon Press, revised edition, p. 111.
6. Frankl, *The Doctor and the Soul,* p. 276.
7. Frankl, *Psychotherapy and Existentialism,* p. 9.
8. *Ibid.,* p. 136.
9. For the most comprehensive recent review and summary of the theological issues and a discerning analysis of the problems see James M. Gustafson, 1968, *Christ and the Moral Life,* New York City, Harper & Row.
10. Langdon Gilkey, 1966: *Shantung Compound,* New York City, Harper & Row.
11. Dietrich Bonhoeffer, 1953: *Letters and Papers From Prison,* New York City, Macmillan.
12. See Richard Rubenstein, 1966: *After Auschwitz*; 1968, *The Religious Imagination,* Bobbs-Merrill and 1970, *Morality and Eros,* New York City, McGraw-Hill Book Company.

5. THE INTEGRATED PERSON

1. Rollo May, 1969: *Love and Will,* New York City, W. W. Norton and Company, p. 97.
2. Rollo May, 1953: *Man's Search for Himself,* New York City, W. W. Norton and Company, pp. 90–93.
3. *Ibid.,* p. 116.
4. *Ibid.,* pp. 174–75.
5. *Ibid.,* pp. 265–69.
6. Rollo May, 1958: "The Origins and Significance of the Existential Movement in Psychology" in Rollo May, Ernest Angel and Henri F. Ellenberger, *Existence: A New Dimension in Psychiatry and Psychology,* New York City, Basic Books.
7. Anders Nygren, 1953: *Agape and Eros,* Philadelphia, The Westminster Press and 1969, New York City, Harper & Row Torchbook.
8. Paul Tillich, 1954: *Love, Power, and Justice,* New York City, Oxford University Press.

9. Reuel L. Howe, 1953: *Man's Need and God's Action,* New York City, Seabury Press.
10. Joseph Fletcher, 1966: *Situation Ethics,* Philadelphia, The Westminster Press, see especially pp. 30, 57, 60–86, 103–6.
11. Jules J. Toner, 1968: *The Experience of Love,* New York City, Corpus Books; James M. Gustafson, 1968, *Christ and the Moral Life,* New York City, Harper & Row, pp. 120–30; and Daniel Day Williams, 1968, *The Spirit and Forms of Love,* New York City, Harper & Row.
12. Joseph Fletcher, *Situation Ethics,* pp. 105–6. For additional comparisons see Denis de Rougemont, 1956, *Love in the Western World,* New York City, Pantheon; Martin C. D'Arcy, 1947, *The Mind and Heart of Love,* New York City, Holt; and Ralph Harper, 1966, *Human Love, Existential and Mystical,* Baltimore, The Johns Hopkins University Press.
13. For an extended analysis of these matters see: Philip Reiff, 1959, *Freud: The Mind of the Moralist,* Garden City, Doubleday and 1966, *The Triumph of the Therapeutic,* New York City, Harper & Row, and David Bakan, 1966, *The Duality of Human Existence,* Chicago, Rand McNally and 1968, *Disease, Pain, and Sacrifice,* Chicago, University of Chicago Press.

6. THE SELF-ACTUALIZING PERSON

1. Abraham H. Maslow, 1954: *Motivation and Personality,* New York City, Harper & Row, p. 340.
2. *Ibid.,* pp. 210–11.
3. Abraham Maslow, 1962: *Toward A Psychology of Being,* Princeton, D. Van Nostrand Company, p. 3.
4. Abraham Maslow, 1964: *Religion, Values, and Peak-Experiences,* Columbus, Ohio, Ohio State University Press, pp. 92–93.
5. Maslow, *Toward A Psychology of Being,* p. 109.
6. Maslow, *Motivation and Personality,* p. 168.
7. Primary examples would be: John Calvin, *Institutes of the Christian Religion,* 2 volumes, ed. J. T. McNeill, Philadelphia,

The Westminster Press, 1960; John Wesley, *John Wesley's Journal* and *A Plain Account of Christian Perfection,* 1953 editions, Naperville, Illinois, Alec Allenson and *Compend of Wesley's Theology,* ed. R. W. Burtner and R. E. Chiles, 1954, Nashville, Abingdon Press; Jonathan Edwards, *Freedom of the Will,* 1957, and *Religious Affections,* 1959, New Haven, Yale University Press and *The Nature of True Virtue,* 1960, University of Michigan Press and *Basic Writings,* New York City, New American Library; J. Gresham Machen, *What Is Faith?, The Christian Faith in the Modern World, Christianity and Liberalism,* Grand Rapids, Eerdmans and *The Virgin Birth of Christ,* Grand Rapids, Baker Book House.

8. Abraham Maslow, *Motivation and Personality,* p. 184.

9. See Frank G. Globe, 1970: *The Third Force: The Psychology of Abraham Maslow,* New York City, Grossman Publishers.

7. SELFHOOD IN PSYCHOLOGY AND RELIGION

1. In particular these recent examples: Seward Hiltner, 1952, *Pastoral Counseling,* 1958, *Preface To Pastoral Theology,* 1959, *The Christian Shepherd,* 1962, *Self-Understanding,* Nashville, Abingdon Press; Donald F. Tweedie, 1961, *Logotherapy and the Christian Faith,* Grand Rapids, Baker Books; James E. Loder, 1966, *Religious Pathology and Christian Faith,* Philadelphia, The Westminster Press; Thomas C. Oden, 1966, *Kerygma and Counseling,* and 1967, *Contemporary Theology and Psychotherapy,* Philadelphia, The Westminster Press; Norman Vincent Peale, 1948, *A Guide To Confident Living,* 1954, *The Power of Positive Thinking,* 1961, *The Tough-Minded Optimist,* Englewood Cliffs, Prentice-Hall.

2. For example, the assignment of a specific date for the end of the world. See Leon Festinger, et al., *When Prophecy Fails,* Minneapolis, The University of Minnesota Press, 1956, and New York City, Harper & Row Torchbooks.

3. Peter Homans, 1970: *Theology After Freud,* Indianapolis, Bobbs-Merrill, pp. 129–30.

4. *Ibid.,* pp. 162–63.
5. *Ibid.,* p. 231.
6. Robert J. Lifton, 1968: *Revolutionary Immortality,* New York City, Random House, p. 152. Also see, "Protean Man," chapter 15 in *History and Human Survival,* 1970, New York City, Random House and *Boundaries: Psychological Man in Revolution,* 1970, New York City, Random House.